20
YEARS

A Concise
Chronology of
events in
Northern Ireland
from 1968-1988

Michael Hall

Island Publications
132, Serpentine Road, Newtownabbey,
Northern Ireland

December, 1988

Printed by Allprint Graphic Services, Belfast.

Introduction

A concise chronology, by its very nature, must omit many items, and when looking at events over the past twenty years in Northern Ireland, it would be impossible to list every march, every political statement, every bombing, and every death. Indeed, the tragedy is that while in the early years each fatality was widely noted, eventually the relentless death toll became only a matter of statistics, and real people in death became just numbers. Except, that is, to the bereaved - as the widow of a murdered policeman said: 'After they die, they will be forgotten, except by those who loved them.'

While acknowledging that my own selection is therefore incomplete, I tried to pick out those events which seemed to be significant in their importance, or which indicated the mood and the feelings within the community at the time. Some years are in fact covered in reasonable depth, others much less so. This is because in some years events seemed to be far-reaching in their impact; in other years, although the death toll continued unabated, within the community itself there was only a weary resignation and political stagnation.

However, I did pick out 1981, the year of the Republican Hunger Strike and Rev. Paisley's 'Third Force', and listed every death attributable to the political situation, to show the unremitting nature of what the community was going through And yet the death toll for that year was less than a quarter than that for 1972, the worst year for sectarian assassinations, so one can imagine the constant community tension there was then, and also how impossible it would have been for me to include every death in this chronology.

Some readers will maybe wonder why certain political and social movements dramatically enter the headlines (for example Rev. Paisley's 'Third Force', the Peace People, Garrett Fitzgerald's 'Crusade'), and then seemingly fade from sight. That's just the nature of things in Northern Ireland: many groups quickly collapse; coalitions form and then hastily fall asunder; movements change direction, or continue to linger on in a less noticeable form.

The inadequacy that I am most conscious of, is with regard to the 'hidden' history of the efforts of ordinary people, striving both as individuals and in groups, to try and bridge the gap between the communities, and even to go further and work for real social change. But while this undercurrent of history is very real, by its nature it is almost impossible to date accurately. Community efforts, even those in which individuals took courageous steps in their attempts to seek a way out of the tragedy that was engulfing their society, never paid much heed to minute-taking, or report-writing, or press statements. I did intend to detail some of these efforts, but when I interviewed the participants their replies showed that the exact day, even the exact month, sometimes the exact part of the year, eluded their memories. I hope that in some other publication I can accord this 'hidden' history the justice it deserves.

Northern Ireland's real tragedy involves a very special section of its society - its children: those who have died, those who have been maimed, those who have been left bereaved, and those who are left mentally scarred by their elders' inability to come together and find a solution. The one thing that unites the 4-year-old girl who died in her father's bobby-trapped car, the 15-month-old baby boy who died in his mother's arms after a bomb blast, the 7-year-old boy killed by a landmine while tending a herd of cows, the 14-year-old girl shot in the head as she peeped through her curtains, the 11-year-old girl killed by a plastic bullet while going for milk, and all the countless other tragedies, is that whatever type of society the adults have conceived for the future, for these children it is already too late.

It is to them that this book is dedicated.

Prelude

26 February 1962 The Irish Republican Army (IRA) border campaign in Northern Ireland, which had begun on **11 December 1956** and during which 6 members of the Royal Ulster Constabulary (RUC), 8 members of the IRA and 4 Republican supporters had been killed, officially ended. That the campaign had failed to gain any support from the northern Catholic population was admitted by the IRA in their cease-fire statement: 'Foremost among the factors motivating this course of action has been the attitude of the general public whose minds have been deliberately distracted from the supreme issue facing the Irish people - the unity and freedom of Ireland.'

September 1962 At a meeting of the IRA Army Council in Dublin, Ruairi O'Bradaigh resigned as Chief-of-Staff, and was replaced by Cathal Goulding.

1963 The 200th anniversary of the birth of Wolfe Tone, one of the founders of Irish Republicanism, was marked by the Republican leadership with the founding of a Wolfe Tone Society as a means to re-evaluate beliefs and strategy following the failure of the border campaign.

January 1964 Conn McCluskey, a Dungannon doctor, and his wife Patricia founded the Campaign for Social Justice, and began to publicise grievances and injustices in Northern Ireland, particularly employment, housing and electoral malpractices against the minority Catholic community.

September 1964 When, during the run-up to a British General Election, an Irish Tricolour was displayed in the Divis Street headquarters of the Republican Party in West Belfast, Rev. Ian Paisley, leader of the Free Presbyterian Church, threatened to remove it if the authorities did not. On the **28th**, when the RUC, armed with sten-guns, revolvers, riot-batons and shields, went to seize the flag they were confronted by more than 2,000 Republican supporters. After the police had smashed down the doors of the headquarters with pickaxes and taken possession of the flag, trouble erupted. Severe rioting continued for another three nights.

14 January 1965 Sean Lemass, Taoiseach (Prime Minister) of the Irish

1

Republic, lunched at Stormont - seat of the Northern Ireland government - at the invitation of Captain Terence O'Neill, Prime Minister of Northern Ireland. Afterwards, the Unionist Party asked Captain O'Neill not to take any similar action on his own initiative without consulting them first.

25 February 1965 Rev. Ian Paisley led a mass rally outside Unionist Party headquarters in Belfast in protest at the meeting between O'Neill and Lemass.

21 January 1966 In London, Rev. Ian Paisley was ejected from Westminster Abbey while taking part in an anti-ecumenical protest.

20 February 1966 Rev. Ian Paisley, speaking in the Ulster Hall, Belfast, warned that 30,000 people from the Republic were expected to come north for the 50th anniversary of the 1916 Easter Rising. On **1 March** he spoke at a rally of the newly-formed Ulster Protestant Volunteers.

22 March 1966 Rev. Ian Paisley went to Rome to protest against the Archbishop of Canterbury's visit to the Pope.

21 May 1966 Belfast newspapers received a statement claiming to be from the Ulster Volunteer Force (UVF), which said: 'From this day we declare war against the IRA and its splinter groups. Known IRA men will be executed mercilessly and without hesitation.'

27 May 1966 A Catholic man, John Scullion, was attacked as he walked along the Falls Road (he died on **11 June**). An anonymous caller to the *Belfast Telegraph* claimed the UVF were responsible.

6 June 1966 Rev. Ian Paisley led a protest march in Belfast against the 'Romeward trend' in the Presbyterian Church. The march was attacked by a Catholic crowd at Cromac Square, but eventually reached Church House, where the marchers shouted abuse at the Governor and Lady Erskine, and at the Moderator of the Presbyterian Church.

26 June 1966 In Belfast, Peter Ward, a Catholic barman, was murdered and two companions injured by gunmen as they left a public house in Malvern Street, off the Protestant Shankill Road. Five members of the UVF, including 'Gusty' Spence, were later charged with the murders of Scullion and Ward. One of the UVF men was alleged to have said after being charged: 'I am sorry

I ever heard tell of that man Paisley.' Rev. Ian Paisley in a statement to the *News Letter* said: 'Like everyone else I deplore and condemn this killing, as all right-thinking people must do. Incitement, direct or indirect, must be treated with the full rigour of the law.'

28 June 1966 The UVF was proscribed by order of the Special Powers Act, under which the IRA was already illegal.

13 August 1966 The Wolfe Tone Societies of Dublin, Belfast and Cork held a conference in Maghera, County Londonderry, attended by, among others, Cathal Goulding and Roy Johnston from the Dublin IRA leadership, some northern IRA leaders, and Conn and Patricia McCluskey. Debate centred around an article written by Anthony Coughlan, but to the eleven northerners present, the ideas expressed were 'alarming, and only one gave the strategy any backing'. (2) (In a further article Coughlan argued that committees should be set up across Northern Ireland 'to organise the maximum number of people at a local level to bring pressure on local authorities, on Stormont, but particularly on Westminster, to wrest so many concessions from O'Neill that he begins to sweat blood'. - *Tuairisc*, **31.9.66**) The following day it was decided to initiate a civil rights crusade, but to drop the Wolfe Tone Society banner and sponsor further meetings to attract a wider spectrum of support.

29 January 1967 The Northern Ireland Civil Rights Association (NICRA) came into being, containing both Protestant and Catholic members, and whose steering committee included members of the Belfast Wolfe Tone Society, trade unionists, communists, moderate reformers, Republicans and a Young Unionist. The demands that NICRA finally adopted as its programme were: (i) one-man-one-vote in local elections; (ii) the removal of gerrymandered boundaries; (iii) laws against discrimination by local government, and the provision of machinery to deal with complaints; (iv) allocation of public housing on a points system; (v) repeal of the Special Powers Act; (vi) disbandment of the 'B' Specials.

7 March 1967 William Craig, Minister of Home Affairs at Stormont, banned the Republican Clubs, under whose name Republicans in the North had circumvented a ban on Sinn Fein, and its newspaper *United Irishman*, in 1964. Republicans held an illegal rally to which NICRA leaders were invited. The inaugural act of NICRA was to denounce the ban and call for the repeal of the Special Powers Act.

June 1967 In his address at the annual Wolfe Tone commemorations at Bodenstown in the Irish Republic, the IRA Chief-of-Staff Cathal Goulding said that the Republican movement should not be so elitist but should join up with other organisations in support of the common ideal, and that in future the use of physical force should only be engaged in when it was 'demanded and supported by the people'.

October 1967 A Sinn Fein internal policy document *Educational Manual Vol III*, written by Roy Johnston, said: 'The major obstacle to the development of radical national ideas in the Six Counties is the lack of any form of communication between the movement and the people... The existence of a ban on the legality of the movement makes the position even more difficult... Both these facts point to the high priority of the struggle for Civil Rights... It is necessary to realise that non-Republican people in the North are not disposed to agitate to get Civil Liberties for Republicans, they have to be involved in their own interests. Which means that if a Civil Liberties movement is to be built in the North, it will have to involve Catholics on the issue of discrimination in housing and jobs, and the Protestant working class on the issue of the local government electoral register which is weighed against them by the property qualification... Force O'Neill to concede more than he wants to do or than he thinks he can dare give without risking overthrow by the more reactionary elements among the Unionists. Demand more than may be demanded by the compromising elements that exist among the Catholic leadership.'

11 December 1967 Jack Lynch, Taoiseach of the Irish Republic, paid a courtesy call on Captain O'Neill at Stormont. He was heckled by Rev. Paisley and his supporters, who shouted 'Keep Ulster Protestant'.

1968

27 April NICRA held a public rally in Armagh to protest at the ban on the Republican Clubs. The Ulster Protestant Volunteers later protested that the Tricolour was displayed at the meeting.

20 May A hostile demonstration by 500 Protestants, carrying placards saying 'O'Neill must go', pelted Captain O'Neill's car with stones and eggs.

20 June Nationalist MP Austin Currie, protesting at what he claimed was unfair housing allocation, and aided by members of the local Republican Club, 'squatted' in a house at Caledon, Co. Tyrone. He was eventually removed by the police.

24 August The-first Civil Rights march took place, sponsored by NICRA but organised by Austin Currie. 2,500 people walked from Coalisland to Dungannon to protest about housing allocation in the area. Stewards, of whom 70 were from the IRA's Northern units, managed to prevent any confrontation between the marchers and a 'counter-demonstration' organised by the Ulster Protestant Volunteers.

8 September NICRA notified the RUC of its intention to stage a march in Derry on **5 October.** NICRA had been invited to sponsor the march by the local Republican and Labour activists in the Derry Housing Action Committee, one of whom, Eamonn McCann, was to admit that their 'conscious, if unspoken, strategy was to provoke the police into over-reaction and thus spark off mass reaction against the authorities'. After the meeting, one of the Derry activists, with either a strong sense of melodrama or a shrewd knowledge of political realities, commented: 'Well, that's it - Stormont is finished.' (3)

30 September The Apprentice Boys of Derry protested to the Minister of Home Affairs about the proposed Civil Rights march, alleging that it was only a 'cover' for a Republican rally. The next day the Apprentice Boys gave notice of an 'Annual Initiation Ceremony' also to be held on **5 October**, covering a similar route to the CRA march. (The Apprentice Boys is a Protestant and Loyalist organisation that commemorates 13 Protestant apprentices who shut the gates of Derry against the forces of the Catholic King James II during the Great Siege in 1688-89.)

3 October William Craig, Minister of Home Affairs, announced a ban on both the planned marches. Derry Labour Party claimed Craig's decision was a 'put-up job', and said they intended to march.

4 October A delegation from NICRA met with the Derry activists and announced that the march was cancelled, but when the Derry representatives stated their intention to proceed, the NICRA Executive finally announced their intention to defy the ban. Activists toured the Catholic working-class areas of the Bogside and Creggan calling on people to 'come out tomorrow

5

and show your contempt for the law'.

5 October The 400 marchers, including local Nationalist and British Labour Party MP's, were halted by a police line at Craigavon Bridge. NICRA speakers then urged the marchers to disperse, saying that their point had been made. After some pushing and shoving, placards were thrown at the police and the latter charged the marchers, hitting out with their batons. As the marchers fled, a second line of RUC met them from behind and batons and water cannon were again used, in full view of TV cameras. One of the marchers, Bernadette Devlin, later described it: 'While everyone was running madly round me, I was standing still - not because I hadn't panicked, but because panic had a different effect on me. I was standing almost paralysed watching the expressions on the faces of the police. Arms and legs were flying everywhere, but what horrified me was the evil delight the police were showing as they beat people down, then beat them again to prevent them from getting up, then trailed them up and threw them on for somebody else to give them a thrashing. It was as though they had been waiting to do it for fifty years.' (4)

9 October Following outbreaks of violence in Derry the Derry Citizens' Action Committee was formed, with Ivan Cooper as Chairman and John Hume as Vice-Chairman. In Belfast, following a sit-down protest by students in Linenhall Street, a meeting was held at Queen's University at which what was to be called the People's Democracy (PD) was formed. The PD, mostly composed of students, ex-students and young workers, was soon to become the most active and left-wing of all the civil rights organisations.

30 October Jack Lynch, Taoiseach of the Irish Republic, at a meeting in London with the British Prime Minister Harold Wilson, told him that he felt partition was the cause of the unrest.

16 November 15,000 people took part in a peaceful Civil Rights march in Derry.

November *United Irishman* said: 'What can we of the Republican movement learn from these happenings? The obvious thing is to leave the Civil Rights people alone... For Republicans or any other group to attempt a takeover would bring about its downfall... The next twelve months will tell the story of the North - whether basic rights can be gained through non-violence or through the use of stronger weapons.' 'If enough pressure is put upon the British government they may be forced to intervene, and the Government of

Ireland Act, which established the Unionists in power, may be turned into a weapon against them.'

22 November   Captain O'Neill announced a 5-point reform programme, consisting of a points system for housing allocation, the appointment of an ombudsman, the reform of local government elections, a review of the Special Powers Act, and the replacement of Londonderry Corporation by the Londonderry Development Commission.

30 November   5,000 Civil Rights marchers, on a legal march, were prevented from passing through Armagh by an unlawful assembly of 1,000 supporters of Rev. Ian Paisley and Major Ronald Bunting, some of whom carried sticks and pipes with sharpened ends. The RUC were unable to clear the counter-demonstrators. Stoning between rival groups occurred afterwards. A few days later the RUC served summonses on Rev. Paisley and Major Bunting for illegal assembly.

2 December   William Craig, in a speech at the Ulster Hall, Belfast, claimed that the Civil Rights movement was bogus, and, with reference to the Irish Republic, said that where you had a Roman Catholic majority you had a lesser standard of democracy.

9 December   Captain O'Neill in a TV speech that began with the words 'Ulster stands at the crossroads', asked: 'What kind of Ulster do you want? A happy and respected province... or a place continually torn apart by riots and demonstrations, and regarded by the rest of Britain as a political outcast?' He appealed to the Civil Rights movement: 'Your voice has been heard, and clearly heard. Your duty now is to take the heat out of the situation.' Following the broadcast 150,000 people sent in letters or telegrams of support. NICRA called for a period of 'truce' without marches or demonstrations.

11 December   Captain O'Neill called upon William Craig to resign, after the latter had disputed his views in a speech the previous day. Craig resigned as Minister of Home Affairs.

12 December   Captain O'Neill received a 'massive' vote of confidence from the Unionist Parliamentary Party.

December   In Strabane Seamus Rodgers, from Donegal Sinn Fein, told a

7

meeting: 'The Civil Rights movement has done more in a few weeks to damage the Unionist structure than decades of IRA activities.'(2)

20 December The PD announced that it intended to make a four-day march from Belfast to Derry commencing on **1 January**. Some Civil Rights leaders expressed opposition to any such march, feeling that O'Neill should be given a breathing space.

31 December Major Ronald Bunting, Commandant of the Loyal Citizens of Ulster, appealed to all those who valued their heritage to 'hinder and harass' the planned PD march.

1969

1 January Forty members of the People's Democracy assembled at Belfast City Hall to begin their 4-day march to Derry. Major Ronald Bunting was also there with a group of his supporters, some of them chanting 'One Teague, no vote'. Outside Antrim hostile and abusive Protestants blocked the marchers' route, and the police, unable to clear a way by foot, eventually took the students to their night-time destination in police tenders.

2 January The PD march resumed but didn't get far as Protestant counter-demonstrators carrying cudgels and sticks had taken over a bridge at Randalstown. Among them was Major Bunting, who later said: 'I told County Inspector Cramsie not to repeat his previous mistake, but to halt the march well out of our way, out of sight. He saw the sense of this right away and stopped them where I directed.'(5) The marchers decided to go in cars, provided by volunteers from around the area, along a diversionary route to Toomebridge, where the march resumed. On the way to Maghera the police again stopped the marchers and ordered a rerouting. Less that two miles along this new route a sizable crowd of Protestants lay in wait. When the marchers insisted on being escorted through this crowd, they were subjected to a shower of nails and bolts. In Maghera groups of Protestants gathered, many armed with broken chair legs and iron staves. Later they smashed windows and wrecked shops.

3 January Outside Dungiven the police again advised the marchers that hostile

8

crowds were gathering ahead and a rerouting would be necessary. The marchers decided to ignore this suggestion, linked arms and forged ahead through the police cordon, only to find no reception awaiting them at all. That night, unknown to the marchers, an unofficial 'guard' was mounted outside their hall by local Republicans and armed IRA members. (6)

4 January As the march approached Burntollet Bridge, a few miles from Derry, it was ambushed by hundreds of Protestants, who first hurled stones and bottles at the marchers, and then assaulted their ranks with sticks and iron bars. Many of the marchers were forced off the road into an adjoining field, where some were beaten up and forced into a river. Many of the marchers were injured by the attackers, whose ranks contained many off-duty 'B' Specials. By the time the marchers reached Derry thousands of local people, who had heard about the ambush, came out to meet them, and were stoned by Protestants on the outskirts of the city. One of the last remaining banners, that of the Belfast Anarchist Group, was seized in an ambush in Irish Street and set on fire. That evening members of the RUC entered the Bogside and, in the words of the Cameron Commission, 'were guilty of misconduct which involved assault and battery, malicious damage to property... and the use of provocative sectarian and political slogans.'

5 January A local 'citizens' army' was formed in the Bogside after the previous night's police action, and barricades were erected. One resident painted 'You are now entering Free Derry' on a gable-end in St. Columb's Street. Captain O'Neill issued a statement claiming the PD march was 'a foolhardy and irresponsible undertaking'. He said: 'We are all sick of marchers and counter-marchers. Enough is enough. We have heard sufficient for now about Civil Rights; let us hear a little about civic responsibility.' The statement made no reference to the conduct of the police.

6 January It was announced that County Inspector Baillie was to head an inquiry into allegations of RUC misconduct during the week-end violence in Derry.

7 January Newry PD announced it would hold a Civil Rights march on the **11th**.

8 January Major Bunting promised 'our biggest yet demonstration' to protest at the planned Civil Rights march in Newry. He called it off on the **10th**.

9 January Roy Bradford, Unionist MP, claimed that the Civil Rights movement was only out to overthrow the government. He said that the five major reforms passed on 22 November had dealt with the root of all 'real or imagined grievances'.

11 January The RUC banned the Civil Rights march from going through the centre of Newry, and police barriers and vehicles blocked Merchant's Quay. A riot developed that the stewards couldn't control and seven police vehicles were overturned, set on fire or else pushed into the canal.

13 January Civil Rights activists expressed the view that the violence at Newry was a setback for the movement. Barry White's article in the *Belfast Telegraph* had the caption: 'March that saw non-violence ideals go up in flames.'

15 January Captain O'Neill announced the setting up of an independent Commission (the Cameron Commission) to inquire into all the violence since 5 October 1968. Newry PD issued a statement analysing the events in the town, and pointed out that when the marchers had arrived at the police barrier, there was a crowd of 200 people already there, who had not been on the march. They asked who these people were.

16 January Harry West, Unionist MP, said that the Civil Rights movement was only a 'cloak' for 'our old traditional enemies'.

30 January A group of 12 Unionist MP's said they would like to see a change in the Party leadership.

3 February Captain O'Neill dissolved the Stormont Parliament, and called a General Election.

6 February The New Ulster Movement was officially launched.

24 February General Election in Northern Ireland. Captain O'Neill was returned, and on the **28th** confirmed as leader by his Party. John Hume was elected for Foyle, and Ivan Cooper for Mid-Derry.

9 March Shots hit a police vehicle in South Armagh. On the **12th** it was announced that police on Border patrol were to be armed. On **12 April** it was further announced that the RUC were to be generally rearmed.

16 March   Leading members of the NICRA executive resigned in protest at 'infiltration' of the movement by 'extremist elements' from the PD.

25 March   Rev. Ian Paisley and Major Bunting began their sentences at Crumlin Road jail in Belfast, having been found guilty of unlawful assembly at Armagh on 30 November.

30 March   The Castlereagh electricity transformer was wrecked by an explosion.   The next day Captain O'Neill announced the part-time mobilisation of 1,000 members of the Ulster Special Constabulary (USC), to guard installations.

4 April The PD began a cross-border march to Dublin, deciding not to physically march through the North, but instead to hold public meetings in Lurgan and Newry.   In Lurgan 18 PD members were arrested after a sit-down.   The march was intended to highlight civil rights injustices North and South.   At the border a PD member protested at the South's censorship laws by producing banned books.   This action alienated some Southern supporters, one of whom stated that it offended 'the republican socialist feelings of a large section of the 26 Counties'. (7)   At one of the marchers' night-time halts John McGuffin and members of the Belfast Anarchist Group suggested that a small party should go in advance to Dublin and walk straight into the traditional Easter Rising commemoration parade as President de Valera was taking the salute from the front of the GPO, and then produce concealed placards.   The idea was abandoned due to the tiredness of the marchers.

7 April The PD march arrived in Dublin.   Some waiting Republican supporters were annoyed when they failed to get the PD members to march in strict 'military' lines through the city centre.

18 April Bernadette Devlin was elected as a Unity candidate in the Mid-Ulster by-election.

19 April Violence erupted in Derry when Paisley supporters stoned Civil Rights supporters.   Police used baton-charges and water cannons against Catholic crowds in the Bogside.   When police sealed off the Bogside, barricades were erected in Rossville Street and petrol bombs thrown at the RUC.   Paisleyites threw stones into the Bogside from the City Walls.   Police were later accused of brutality, including entering the house of Samuel Devenny and beating him up in front of his family (he died on **17 July**).

20 April A large explosion smashed the main pipeline between the Silent Valley reservoir and Belfast. An electricity pylon in County Armagh was damaged by an explosion. After a Civil Rights rally in West Belfast a crowd attacked Hastings Street RUC station. Later nine post offices were set on fire and two buses were burned. In Newry Civil Rights supporters attacked the police station, and barricades were erected in Dungannon. In Derry John Hume, after a meeting with local people, arranged for a group of civic leaders to request that the police withdraw from the Bogside. Robert Porter, Minister of Home Affairs, agreed, once he had been assured that peace would be preserved.

23 April The Unionist Parliamentary Party voted, by 28 votes to 22, to adopt universal adult franchise in local government elections.

24 April An explosion shattered the main pipeline from Lough Neagh to Belfast. William Craig said: 'The people of Ulster will not surrender their Parliament without a fight. What we see today on the streets of our province - the disorders - will look like a Sunday school picnic if Westminster tries to take our Parliament away.'

25 April An explosion damaged a pipeline at Annalong, County Down. Police sources said that these recent bombings 'were caused by people working to an IRA plan'.

27 April In the *Sunday Times* the 'Insight' team wrote: 'The monster of sectarian violence is well out of its cage. The issue now is no longer Civil Rights or even houses and jobs. The issue is now whether the state should exist and who should have the power, and how it should be defended; and this is an issue on which the wild men on both sides have sworn for 40 years, frequently in blood, that they will never back down.'

28 April Captain O'Neill resigned as leader of the Unionist Party. In the Protestant working-class Shankill Road area of Belfast celebration bonfires were lit.

1 May Major James Chichester-Clark was elected Northern Ireland Prime Minister.

5 May Captain O'Neill said: 'If you treat Roman Catholics with due consideration and kindness, they will live like Protestants, in spite of the authoritarian nature of their Church.'

6 May An amnesty was announced for all those charged or convicted as a result of the political protests.

16 May Beginning of three nights of trouble between police and Catholic crowds at Hooker street in Belfast.

18 May NICRA gave the government six weeks to issue a timetable of reforms, otherwise they would resume street demonstrations.

24 May After more violence at Hooker Street, a Citizens' Action Committee was formed to try and disperse 'drunks', in an effort to stop the rioting. There were allegations made of police misconduct.

May In the *New Left Review* Eamonn McCann admitted that the Civil Rights campaign, instead of uniting the two communities as originally hoped, was dividing them more than ever: 'We keep saying parrot-like that we are fighting on working-class issues for working-class unity... It is a lot of pompous nonsense... The consciousness of the people who are fighting in the streets at the moment is sectarian and bigoted... Everyone applauds loudly when one says in a speech that we are not sectarian, we are fighting for the rights of all Irish workers, but really that's because they see this as the new way of getting at the Protestants.'

June The Chairman of NICRA, Frank Gogarty, visited Cathal Goulding in Dublin to ask if the IRA could be relied upon for protection if the violence in the North continued to worsen, but left dissatisfied with the answer he received. (2)

14 June After a Commemoration parade for the Irish socialist James Connolly was banned from entering the centre of Belfast, John McKeague, Chairman of the Shankill Defence Association, addressed a crowd at the Central Library, telling them: 'Belfast has no time for James Connolly.'

19 June Opposition MP's at Stormont in a joint statement said they thought the Government's timetable of reforms was 'reasonable'.

28 June Differences emerged among Civil Rights leaders at a rally in Strabane, when speakers urging the merits of accepting the government's reform programme were accused of 'selling out'.

5 July At a Civil Rights rally in Newry, the Secretary of Newry CRA claimed that a Catholic Mafia had ruled Newry for years and nepotism was widely practised.

12 July During the annual Orange celebrations (when Protestants celebrate the victory of King William of Orange over King James II at the Battle of the Boyne in 1690) sectarian clashes erupted in Belfast after Protestant bands were jeered at and pelted with bottles from Unity Flats, the small Catholic working-class enclave at the bottom of the Protestant Shankill Road. In Derry youths stoned Orangemen, and rioting continued throughout the night.

13 July Heavy rioting in Derry. In Dungiven a man who was knocked down when police baton-charged a Catholic crowd later died.

14 July On both the Protestant and Catholic sides of the Crumlin Road in Belfast residents formed defence groups, while police in riot gear stood between rival crowds.

15 July The Minister for Home Affairs, Robert Porter, announced that, because of the disturbances of the past 48 hours, several hundred members of the USC - to be armed only with batons - were being called up to strengthen the RUC.

20 July The Derry Citizens' Action Committee, dominated by John Hume, was superseded by the more militant Derry Citizens' Defence Association, dominated by local Republicans such as Sean Keenan. Its purpose was to organise the defence of the Bogside in the event of attack on 12 August, when the Apprentice Boys were to hold their annual march through Derry. In the following weeks barricade material was stored close to all entrances to Catholic working-class areas.

21 July Most of the committee of Armagh CRA resigned in protest at the PD's influence.

26 July After their march in Enniskillen had been banned, 37 PD members were taken into custody when they picketed the RUC station and staged a sit-down.

2 August Following rumours that Catholics from Unity Flats in Belfast had attacked a parade of Junior Orangemen, a Protestant crowd tried to attack the Flats. Police were unable to prevent most of the windows being smashed. The RUC came under attack from both sides. When police reinforcements arrived they baton-charged the Protestant crowd back along the Shankill Road. Sectarian clashes occurred between Catholic residents of Hooker Street on one side of the Crumlin Road and Protestant residents of Disraeli Street on the other. Intimidation was used by both sides to force the evacuation of homes. The RUC were attacked with stones by Protestants and petrol-bombs by Catholics.

3 August When a hostile Protestant crowd was prevented from attacking Unity Flats, they rioted and looted shops. In Hooker Street Catholic residents prepared a trench and barricades to resist invasion and threw petrol-bombs at the police.

4 August The violence continued in Belfast, and the police prevented Protestants from attacking Hooker Street. Members of the USC went on patrol carrying batons. The Shankill Defence Association in a statement condemned the use of water cannon against local people, and said: 'We make it clear the police are no longer our friends and can never expect the help of Ulster Loyalists again.'

10 August In Derry appeals for calm and restraint during the forthcoming Apprentice Boys' parade were made. The Chairman of Derry Citizens' Defence Association said they hoped to avoid any sectarian trouble, but stated that the Bogside would be defended.

12 August The annual Apprentice Boys parade went off peacefully until the afternoon when youths from the Bogside stoned it as it passed through Waterloo Place. Efforts by local leaders to calm the youths failed and police finally baton-charged the crowd. Barricades were thrown up but police breached these with an armoured car and entered the Bogside. Petrol bombs were thrown at them from the top of Rossville Flats. What would become known as the 'Battle of the Bogside' had begun. A crowd of Protestants stoned Catholic homes over the heads of the police. The RUC were authorised to use CS gas - for the first time in the UK. In the evening crowds attacked RUC stations in Coalisland, Strabane and Newry.

13 August The state of siege continued in the Bogside, with Rosemount RUC station set on fire by petrol-bombers, and sectarian clashes occurred in Little James Street. In Belfast, in response to requests by the Bogsiders to relieve the pressure on them, RUC stations were attacked and barricades erected in Catholic areas of West Belfast. The Republic's Taoiseach, Jack Lynch, said on TV that he wanted the United Nations to send in a peace-keeping force immediately. He had arranged for Irish Army field hospitals to be set up near the border. In Derry rioting continued all night.

14 August Bernadette Devlin MP, who was in the Bogside throughout the siege, called on the British Prime Minister, Harold Wilson, to organise a constitutional conference and settle the Irish question 'once and for all'. A general mobilisation of the 'B' Specials was ordered; some of them arrived alongside the exhausted police carying pick handles and cudgels. As A.T.Q. Stewart described it: 'After 48 hours a scene appeared in Derry which no-one in Northern Ireland could remember seeing before... Against a backdrop of blazing buildings, small groups of exhausted policemen huddled in doorways or lay in the streets, their faces streaked with blood and dirt, their tunics torn and even burned, like the weary survivors of some desperate and costly offensive.'(8) After a request for the assistance of troops had been agreed to by the British Home Secretary, James Callaghan, the British Army took over security duties in the city centre at 5 pm and the RUC withdrew. In Belfast crowds faced each other along some of the 'mixed' streets linking the Protestant Shankill and Catholic Falls Road. The Protestants eventually invaded the Catholic area, and began burning homes. The mob was met by gunfire from a group of local IRA men who had taken up positions, with the small handful of guns they could muster, on the roof of St. Comgall's School. Six people died by shooting during the night, including a child who was killed sheltering under his bed when the police opened up on Divis Flats (at the bottom of the Falls Road) with the heavy machine-guns mounted on their armoured cars.

15 August British troops took up duty in Belfast at 5 pm, but were unable to prevent most of Bombay Street being burned down by Protestants. To the disgust of some leading Republicans the troops were welcomed in Catholic areas of Belfast and Derry, but some Catholic refugees took trains to the Irish Republic. In Dublin a hostile demonstration took place outside the British Embassy.

16 August Leading Belfast Republican, Jim Sullivan, founded the Central Citizens' Defence Committee (CCDC), its central committee being made

made up of about thirty delegates from other defence groupings in the Catholic working-class areas of Belfast.

17 August The Derry Citizens' Defence Committee said that before the barricades would come down their demands must be met; their long-term demands included the abolition of Stormont and the disbandment of the 'B' Specials.

19 August 'The Downing Street Declaration' issued by the British Prime Minister Harold Wilson and Major Chichester-Clark stated that it was vital that the momentum of internal reform should be maintained. In Dublin Cathal Goulding, Chief of Staff of the IRA, said that volunteers had been active in the North defending Catholic areas. Local people in West Belfast weren't so impressed, and slogans were soon to appear on walls saying: 'IRA - I Ran Away.' In Derry, posters of Goulding's statement were torn down in disgust by local people.

21 August Major Chichester-Clark announced the setting up of a Commission under Lord Hunt to inquire into the structure of the RUC and USC. Rev. Ian Paisley said: 'Whitehall has already written the obituary of the 'B' Specials.'

22 August In New York, Bernadette Devlin said that the barricades would stay up until the Unionist Government had fallen.

24 August A meeting of discontented IRA men took place in Andersonstown, Belfast; they decided they would have to move against the Belfast brigade command, and then try to replace Goulding's Dublin leadership.

27 August The British Home Secretary, James Callaghan, visited Catholic and Protestant areas of Belfast. Mr. Justice Scarman was appointed to head a tribunal of inquiry into the recent disturbances.

28 August James Callaghan was given a warm welcome in Catholic and Protestant areas of Derry.

29 August A joint communique was issued regarding the speeding up of the reform programme. The following day it was announced that a Community Relations Board would be set up.

September *United Irishman* said: 'The risen people of the North... who would have thought that their ultimate victory would be so great? The spirit and fire of Republicanism has lighted the way to final victory, which cannot now be far away. The rock of Unionism is split to the foundations and to have caused the split is the greatest and most historic achievement of the Civil Rights Movement.'

2 September Protestants in Belfast erected barricades in protest against the continued existence of Catholic barricades.

4 September In Belfast 1,000 soldiers demolished some of the barricades across main arterial roads in Catholic and Protestant districts.

5 September Troops fired CS gas at a hostile gathering of Protestants in Belfast, after the Army had removed a Protestant barricade.

7 September In Belfast troops and residents took down some barricades in the Falls Road area.

8 September After a Protestant vigilante was shot dead in the Oldpark Road area of Belfast, Catholic familes were intimidated out of their homes.

9 September The General Officer Commanding (GOC NI), General Sir Ian Freeland, announced that troops would begin erecting a 'Peace Line'.

12 September The Cameron Report received general acceptance.

14 September A meeting took place in Belfast between Northern IRA dissidents and individuals from the Irish Republic. There had been several of these meetings, which had included prominent Dublin businessmen, members of Taca (the Fianna Fail fund-raising group), and Captain James Kelly of Irish Army Intelligence. The theme of the meetings was similar: the Northern men would receive funding for arms if they would form a separate Northern command, and abandon political operations in the Republic.

15 September After the Army removed some Catholic barricades, local people later rebuilt them. Residents expressed their annoyance to Dr. Philbin, Catholic Bishop of Down and Conor, when he asked the people to take the barricades down. Over the next week all remaining barricades were taken down in Belfast and Derry.

22 September At a meeting of the IRA's Belfast Command sixteen armed men stormed in. They accused the Belfast leadership of failing to protect the local population, and said that they were taking over. A compromise was reached but it was clear that disaffection was widespread and increasing.

27 September Troubled erupted in Belfast when Protestant football supporters stoned troops guarding Unity Flats. Rioting, in which the Army used CS gas, went on into the early hours of the next morning.

28 September Barricades went up in the Falls Road area again and the Army used CS gas against rioters. More trouble erupted on the Shankill Road, with shots being fired at soldiers.

1 October The GOC NI met with leaders of the Catholic community in Belfast.

4 October Violence erupted in working-class areas of East Belfast between Protestants and the British Army. On the Shankill Road a crowd of Protestants was stopped from getting near Unity Flats.

10 October The Hunt Report recommended the disbandment of the 'B' Specials and the formation of a new part-time force (later called the Ulster Defence Regiment) under the control of the GOC. The Inspector-General of the RUC, Anthony Peacocke, resigned and was replaced by Sir Arthur Young as Chief Constable. While Civil Rights supporters praised the report, angry Protestants roamed the Shankill Road in Belfast.

11 October In extensive rioting on the Shankill Road a policeman was shot dead, and snipers opened up on the police and the Army. When the Army was ordered to return fire, two civilians were killed. In their newspaper *Free Citizen* the PD later said: 'We do not rejoice when any section of the working class is beaten off the streets by the army. The army is here to protect the interests of the British ruling elite, an elite which has as little interest in the fate of the people on the Shankill as it has in the people on the Falls.'

12 October Army searches took place in the Shankill area. Major Chichester-Clark appealed on TV for the Protestant community to keep calm. Military Police patrols became the first security forces to enter 'Free Derry' since the August disturbances. At a PD meeting Michael Farrell said: 'Now that all the Civil Rights demands have been met, we must work further into the future... The PD's objectives can only be obtained by the ousting of both

Tory governments (North and South) and the establishment of an Irish Socialist Republic.'(7)

15 October William Craig said that 'Ulster stands at the brink of civil war'. Unarmed RUC patrols recommenced in the Bogside in Derry (and returned to the Falls Road, Belfast, two days later).

25 October William Craig suggested that there could be a federal solution to the Irish problem, but within the context of the UK.

19 November The Ulster Defence Regiment Bill received an unopposed second reading at Westminster. Civil Rights activists had been expressing scepticism about the new force, some claiming it would be just the 'B' Specials under another name.

5 December A Protestant, connected with the proscribed UVF, was found guilty of causing the explosions at Castlereagh, Kilmore and Lough Neagh, and on the **15th** John McKeague of the Shankill Defence Association and 9 other men were also remanded in custody charged with conspiring to cause explosions.

29 December The *Irish Press*, a Dublin-based newspaper, announced a split within the IRA. A group of dissidents had broken with the Dublin leadership and established a new command. (This became the 'Provisional' IRA, with Sean MacStiofain as Chief-of-Staff. The existing leadership would become know as the 'Officials', with the Republican Clubs as their political counterpart.) The dissidents later said their discontentment with the Goulding leadership was due to: (i) the leadership's recognition of Westminster, Stormont and Leinster House; (ii) their extreme socialist ideas; (iii) the internal methods being used within the Movement; (iv) the failure to give maximum defence to the Northern Catholic population; (v) the campaigning to retain Stormont instead of seeking its abolition.

Death toll for the year: 12 civilians and 1 RUC.

1970

11 January At the Sinn Fein ard fheis Sean MacStiofain seized a microphone and declared his allegiance to the new Provisional Army Council, then he and about one-third of the 257 delegates walked out to reconvene their own conference.

24/27 January Four nights of rioting on the Shankill Road, Belfast. Protestant crowds repeatedly tried to break through to Catholic areas.

7 February NICRA held demonstrations throughout Northern Ireland in protest against the Public Order (Amendment) Act, which had been passed on **5th**.

18 February John McKeague and his co-defendants were found not guilty of conspiring to blow up the pipeline at Dunadry the previous April. There was an explosion not far from the courtroom, which was later claimed by the UVF (they were also to explode a bomb near the home of the Nationalist MP Austin Currie on **7 March**).

18 March Five Unionist MP's (Desmond Boal, John McQuade, William Craig, Harry West and Dr. Norman Laird) were expelled from the party for refusing to support a motion of confidence in the government.

31 March/2 April What were to become known as the 'Ballymurphy Riots' erupted on the Springfield Road in Belfast. Catholic crowds attacked the Protestant estate of New Barnsley. Vigilantes and local Republicans attempted to prevent youths - some of whom were to style themselves 'the Ballymurphy young hooligans' - from rioting. Troops used CS gas and sent in snatch-squads to arrest troublemakers. Protestant children were evacuated from the nearby Springmartin estate. Cardinal Conway appealed for peace. The GOC NI warned that petrol-bombers could be shot dead.

17 April Rev. Ian Paisley won the Stormont by-election at Bannside.

21 April The Alliance Party was formed.

30 April The Ulster Special Constabulary was finally 'stood down' and their duties transferred to the new Ulster Defence Regiment (UDR), which had come officially into being on **1 January**.

9 May Rioting at Flax street on the Crumlin Road in Belfast went on into early morning. The following day there was rioting in the New Lodge Road and Tiger Bay areas of Belfast, again going on into early morning.

16 May Rioting in the Ardoyne and Lower North Street areas of Belfast.

28 May Charles Haughey and Neil Blaney, who had been dismissed from their ministerial posts in the government of the Irish Republic on the **6th**, were charged with conspiring to illegally import arms.

2 June Rioting on the Shankill Road, Belfast, following which allegations were made that the troops chased young people into houses which were then wrecked.

18 June United Kingdom General Election. The Unionist Party lost one seat to Rev. Ian Paisley, another to Frank McManus, Independent.

26 June In Derry 3 members of the Provisional IRA and 2 children were killed when a bomb went off prematurely in a house in the Creggan. (2)

27 June Rioting in Whiterock area of Belfast. In the Ardoyne area gunmen opened up on a Protestant crowd, killing 3 of them. The news of this spread quickly and in East Belfast Protestants began to burn houses in the Short Strand area. A group of Provisionals took up positions in the grounds of St. Matthew's Church, and in the ensuing gun battle one of the IRA men and three Protestants were killed. 200 civilians were injured in the weekend of violence. The PD, in a statement, later said: 'The week-end incidents also show that sectarianism is not the monopoly of the Orange Order. Catholic bigotry and direct action to exploit sectarianism was rampant. Socialism must remain clearly opposed to the reactionary policies of the Green as well as the Orange militants. No one can be blasted into Socialism.'

30 June Legislation was passed providing mandatory 6-month prison sentences for rioters. It was partially repealed on **17 December**.

1 July Reginald Maudling, the British Home Secretary, made a brief visit to the province; on the plane going back to London he is reported to have said: 'For

God's sake bring me a large Scotch. What a bloody awful country.'(6)

2 July Rev. Ian Paisley was suspended from Stormont after angry exchanges. On his way out of the Chamber he said to the Sergeant-at-Arms: 'If you lend me your sword I will decapitate a few of these people before I leave.'

3 July When troops searched a house in Balkan Street in the Lower Falls Road area of Belfast a crowd confronted them. Serious rioting started, and hundreds of troops were rushed to the area, which was then sealed off. The episode that followed was to become known as the 'Falls Curfew', and the Army maintained the curfew for 34 hours. The Official IRA decided to take on the Army and in the gun battles 3 civilians were killed. Except for a restricted period allowed for shopping, the residents were not allowed out of their homes, as the soldiers carried out a house-by-house search, some of them axeing down doors, ripping up floorboards, destroying furniture and smashing religious statuettes in the process. 1,600 canisters of CS gas were fired, and a local priest said that the women of the area were 'white-faced with panic'. 1,000 women from surrounding areas marched in carrying milk and bread.

5 July Gerry Fitt, Republican Labour MP, and Paddy Devlin, NI Labour Party MP, flew to London to complain about the alleged looting and abusive behaviour of the troops during the search.

14 July Although the traditional Orange parades passed off without incident, 1,500 people had crossed the Border to stay in refugee camps in the Republic.

16 July A no-warning explosion in Belfast city centre injured 30 people, 2 seriously.

23 July Anthony Roche was arrested for throwing two CS gas canisters into the Chamber of the House of Commons at Westminster. He had shouted: 'How do you like that, you bastards? Now you know what it's like in Belfast!'

31 July After serious rioting in the Catholic New Lodge area of Belfast British soldiers shot dead a youth who they claimed had a petrol bomb. The rioting continued over the next few nights, during which the Army used a new weapon - rubber bullets. There was trouble also during the youth's funeral on **3 August**.

4 August Paddy Devlin MP claimed that 'the Army are deliberately provoking trouble'. 'They are behaving like a conquering army of medieval times.'

5 August Further rioting in Belfast and Derry.

8 August William Craig called for internment without trial.

11 August Two RUC officers were killed when they went to examine a booby-trapped car near Crossmaglen in South Armagh.

21 August The Social Democratic and Labour Party (SDLP), was formed under the leadership of Gerry Fitt. It included John Hume, Paddy Devlin, and Austin Currie. It saw the reunification of Ireland by consent as a primary goal.

26 September Rioting on the Shankill Road, Belfast, with 300 people injured. It continued next day when crowds laid seige to an Army post. When the disturbances went on into a third day the Northern Ireland Prime Minister, Major Chichester-Clark, described them as 'utter folly'.

3 October Local Shankill residents opened an unoffical inquiry into the recent trouble. Representatives of NICRA attended as observers. The final report, issued on **24 November**, accused the Military Police of acting irresponsibly and aggressively (the Army rejected these findings). The PD paper, *Free Citizen,* commented: 'The report has no sectarian hysterics, indicating that fewer working-class people on the Shankill are taken in by Paisley's sectarian rantings that is often supposed. Indeed, the report of the Peoples' Tribunal is a good deal less concerned with sectarian attitudes than the recent publication of the CCDC, *Law and Orders.*'

10 October A weekend of rioting in Derry. Troops used CS gas.

24 October The PD held a rally at the City Hall in Belfast, against increased bus fares. They had collected 50,000 signatures for a petition.

1 November After nights of rioting in the Ardoyne area of Belfast, the CCDC condemned the throwing of grenades and missiles at the Army. Dr. Philbin, Catholic Bishop of Down and Conor, said that it was the local people who were the victims.

18 November In a major statement the CCDC warned that violence would only damage the cause of justice in Ireland.

21 November Rev. Ian Paisley called upon his followers to support William Craig and Harry West and sweep 'the government out of office'.

28 November A NICRA rally in Enniskillen passed off peacefully. The SDLP had decided not to attend, saying that street demonstrations at this time could do more harm than good.

19 December In Belfast at a Sinn Fein public meeting in Ardoyne, speakers urged local youths to join the Republican movement and condemned the 'infiltration of the district by a Communist element'.

Death toll for the year: 23 civilians, and 2 RUC

1971

17 January Dr. Philbin, Bishop of Down and Conor, in a sermon in Ballymurphy, which had seen a week of rioting, preached against membership of secret organisations, and said that no-one was bound to obey 'immoral orders'.

21 January Ballymurphy women marched to Dr. Philbin's home in protest at his sermon.

25 January 170 delegates to the Ulster Unionist Council called for Major Chichester-Clark's resignation.

4 February The GOC NI, commenting on recent rioting, claimed they were the responsibility of the Provisional IRA, and went on to name 5 men as leading members (he didn't reveal that the Army had been holding meetings with these men). The rioting continued and on the **6th** the first British soldier to die in the recent 'troubles' was killed by machine-gun fire; another victim was the first member of the Provisionals to be killed by the British Army.

7 February Major Chichester-Clark said on TV: 'Northern Ireland is at war with the Irish Republican Army Provisionals.'

9 February Five civilians were killed when a BBC Land Rover was blown up by a land-mine as it drove to the transmitter at Brougher Mountain, County Tyrone.

19 February Jack Lynch, Taoiseach of the Irish Republic, said: 'Where it can be shown that attitudes embodied in our laws and constitution give offence to liberty of conscience then we are prepared to see what can be done to harmonize our views, so that a new kind of Irish society may be created equally agreeable to North and South.'

24 February Major Chichester-Clark welcomed Mr. Lynch's speech, and suggested that the Irish government should drop its claim to have jurisdiction over Northern Ireland.

1 March Jack Lynch said that the Irish Republic's constitutional claim to the North was fundamental and could not be abandoned.

2 March The CCDC condemned the recent shooting dead of two policemen by gunmen.

8 March Gun battles, kidnappings and beatings took place between Official and Provisional IRA members, and left one Provisional dead. The British Army said they would only interfere if innocent people were suffering.

9 March Members of the Provisional IRA lured 3 off-duty Scottish soldiers (two of them brothers, aged 17 and 18) from a pub, and then murdered them on the outskirts of Belfast. Revulsion throughout the province was intense.

12 March 4,000 shipyard workers and shop stewards marched through Belfast demanding that internment be introduced.

20 March Major Chichester-Clark resigned after failing to get the security measures he demanded from the British government. Brian Faulkner was elected Northern Ireland Prime Minister on the **23rd**.

24 May In Belfast, an explosion seriously injured people at the Mountainview Tavern on the Shankill Road. The Official IRA condemned it as the work of 'sectarian bigots'.

26

25 May A soldier died trying to protect children when he threw himself onto a bomb that was flung into Springfield Road Army Post.

28 May In *Free Citizen*, the PD said: 'The last week has seen the introduction of terrorism against civilians on a major scale. The bombs in the British Legion Hall in Suffolk and the pub on the Shankill Road were aimed at, or took no account of, the lives of civilians. There is only one argument which could explain the attacks on civilians. Both the British Legion Hall and Mountainview Bar are in predominantly Protestant districts. There are people on the fringes of both the Civil Rights and Republican movements who habitually refer to their Protestant fellow-Irishmen as 'planters' and talk of driving them into the sea. We can have nothing but contempt for those who would try to build a Republic on the bodies of dead or maimed Protestant Irishmen. For the only Republic that can be established today is the Workers' Republic - and it can only be built with the aid of those very Protestant workers whom these men seek to murder.'

4 June Brian Faulkner said that lack of civil rights was not the reason behind the terrorism, but the desire to create an all-Ireland Republic.

16 June Belfast Corporation Housing Committee finally gave way to the residents of the lower Shankill Road who had refused to move into 2 blocks of flats. The flats were eventually demolished.

21 June At Stormont Brian Faulkner said he proposed to set up three new Parliamentary Committees, and that the Opposition should provide chairmen for two of them. Paddy Devlin said the proposals 'showed plenty of imagination', and John Hume said: 'It should be made clear to all people today who say that no change has taken place, that this is simply not true. There have been changes in this community.'

30 June The Provisional IRA's bombing campaign was gathering momentum: there had been 37 major explosions in April, 47 in May and 50 in June.

8 July On the fourth night of rioting in Derry two men, who the Army claimed were armed, were shot dead.

12 July Ten early-morning bombs went off along the route to be taken by the traditional Orange parade in Belfast. In Derry John Hume said the SDLP would withdraw from Stormont unless there was an impartial inquiry into the deaths of the two Derry men. When this wasn't forthcoming, they withdrew on the **16th**.

9 August Following a day of serious rioting throughout Belfast the Government introduced Internment and the Army detained 342 men in early morning swoops. Most of those interned were from the Official IRA; the Provisionals claimed they had been alerted and few of their members were lifted. There was a violent reaction in Catholic working-class areas, barricades were erected, and in the Republic refugee camps were opened. A unit of the Official IRA led by Joe McCann took over Inglis's Bakery in the Markets area of Belfast on the **10th** and a gun battle was waged against the British Army. By the **12th** 22 people had been killed in the worst violence seen since 1969. Over 240 houses were burned out in the Ardoyne area, and many Catholic and Protestant families were forced to flee their homes.

12 August In the Republic the Taoiseach, Jack Lynch, said that 'The Stormont regime must be brought to an end.' In Protestant working-class areas of Belfast a leaflet was distributed which said: 'Being convinced that the enemies of the Faith and Freedom are determined to destroy the State of Northern Ireland and thereby enslave the people of God, we call on all members of our loyalist institutions, and other responsible citizens, to organise themselves immediately into platoons of twenty under the command of someone capable of acting as a sergeant. A structure of command is already in existence and the various platoons will eventually be linked in a co-ordinated effort.'

15 August Opposition MP's announced they would organise a campaign of mass civil disobedience.

21 August The Provisional IRA announced plans for the formation of a 9-county Ulster Parliament, 'Dail Uladh'.

31 August There were now Protestant vigilante groups and defence associations in the Shankill, Woodvale, Ormeau, Carrick, Donegall Pass, Hammer, Newtownabbey, Abbots Cross, Woodburn, Lisburn Road, Seymour Hill, Suffolk, Castlereagh, Beersbridge, Upper Woodstock and Dundonald areas. In **September** a founder-member of Woodvale Defence Association, Charles Harding Smith, brought them all together under a central council, the Ulster Defence Association (UDA). (9)

4 September Ruairi O'Bradaigh, President of Provisional Sinn Fein, said that the death of a 17-month-old girl, during an attack on an Army patrol the previous day, was one of the hazards of urban guerrilla warfare.

7 September As the bombings and deaths continued, NICRA said that a policy of random bombings and shootings had no relevance to the struggle for justice and reform in the North. There had been over 100 bombings and 35 violent deaths in August alone.

12 September In a statement Cardinal Conway asked 'who wanted to bomb a million Protestants into a United Ireland?'

24 September Statistics estimated that 2,000 familes had left their homes due to intimidation since Internment was introduced.

28 September Rev. Ian Paisley said that an Ulster Loyalist Civil Defence Corps would be set up to oppose the IRA.

29 September A bomb at the Four Step Inn, on the Shankill Road, Belfast, killed 2 people and injured 20.

30 September Rev. Ian Paisley and Desmond Boal announced the formation of a new political party, the Democratic Unionist Party (DUP).

4 October The new Northern Ireland Housing Executive took over from the Housing Trust.

6 October Ruairi O'Bradaigh, President of Provisional Sinn Finn, denied that the IRA's bombing campaign was intended to provoke Protestants.

10 October A peace rally in Botanic Gardens, Belfast, was attended by 4,000 people.

24 October As gun battles and violence continued (over 70 people had now died since Internment), Ruairi O'Bradaigh, at the Sinn Fein ard fheis, said that the most desirable prelude to a 32-county Republic would be to make the North ungovernable and to destroy Stormont. He said they had now gone over to the offensive.

2 November After armed men planted a bomb in the Red Lion public house in

Belfast, and told the customers they had 10 seconds to get out, 3 people were killed and 36 injured in the subsequent explosion.

5 November In Belfast, a 'mission of mercy' was set up in Ballymurphy estate by Mother Theresa of Calcutta.

16 November The Compton Commision, set up to investigate allegations of brutality following Internment, found evidence of ill-treatment. It also transpired that some of the internees had been used as guinea pigs in sensory deprivation experiments where they were hooded, deprived of sleep and food, and subjected to constant unidentifiable background noises intended to disorient them. In Belfast 9 men escaped from the Crumlin Road prison by throwing rope ladders over a wall.

21 November The Northern Resistance Committee, composed of PD and Provisional Sinn Fein, was set up in Omagh, County Tyrone.

4 December A Loyalist bomb at McGurk's bar in North Queen Street, Belfast, killed 15 people.

11 December An explosion at a furniture store on the Shankill Road, Belfast, killed 2 children and 2 adults.

12 December An Offical IRA squad, sent to destroy the home of Senator Jack Barnhill in County Tyrone, killed him when he offered resistance.

Death toll for the year: 114 civilians, 43 Army and 16 RUC and UDR.

1972

1 January The *Belfast Telegraph* said: 'If it is true that the darkest hour precedes the dawn, then Northern Ireland may hope for streaks of light in the sky in 1972. At times the year just past could hardly have seemed worse. The turning-point must come soon... This is the year of decision, when Ulster must decide if it is to be peace or war, a hope of progress or the prospect of a steep descent into the morass.'

2 January At an anti-internment rally in Falls Park, Belfast, Austin Currie, SDLP, said: 'I have no doubt that within the next six or seven months Brian Faulkner and his rotten Unionist system will have been smashed. I say to Maudling: Why the hell should we talk to you? We are winning and you are not.'

3 January 62 people were seriously injured by a no-warning bomb in Callender Street, Belfast.

4 January Brian Faulkner said to the London *Times* that he saw the possibility of a Protestant backlash 'the like of which has never been seen or envisaged'.

17 January 7 detainees escaped from the prison ship 'Maidstone', anchored in Belfast Harbour, by swimming ashore.

18 January The Provisional IRA murdered a Protestant who was a witness in a hi-jacking case.

30 January 'Bloody Sunday'. British paratroopers shot dead 13 men (7 of them under nineteen) after a protest rally in Derry. The Army claimed they were fired on first, but local people strenuously denied this. The IRA in Derry stated that there had been no action by them. A government statement asserted that four of the dead men were on the security forces' wanted list (this was later retracted), and gave a detailed list of the 'gunmen' and 'nail-bombers' who had been shot. The subsequent Widgery tribunal was unable to substantiate that a single one of the men had carried arms or belonged to the IRA. The Londonderry city coroner at the end of the inquest (**21 August**) said: 'They were shooting at innocent people. It was sheer unadulterated murder.' A priest from the Bogside, Father Edward Daly, described his own experience: 'Alarm grew when the armoured car kept coming on. It suddenly dawned on people that this was something different. I remember a young boy laughing at me. I'm not a very graceful runner - that was the only reason I could think he was laughing. He was very cheery... The next thing he suddenly gasped and threw his hands up in the air and fell on his face... There was a terrible lot of blood. We pulled up his jersey and there was a massive bloody hole... He asked me, 'Am I going to die?' and I said 'No', but I administered the last rites. The gunfire started up again and a bullet struck quite close to me. I lay flat and remember trying to talk to the wounded lad and calm him. He was getting confused and I can remember him holding my hand and squeezing it. We all wept... We got him to the top of the street. I kneeled beside him and told him, 'Look son, we've got you out.' But he was dead. He was very youthful looking, just in his seventeenth year but only looked about twelve... He had a baby face...' (10)

31 January In the Irish Republic the Taoiseach Jack Lynch announced a day of national mourning. John Hume, SDLP, said that it was now 'a United Ireland or nothing'. At Westminster Bernadette Devlin physically attacked Reginald Maudling in the House of Commons.

2 February In Dublin the British Embassy was burned down by an angry crowd.

12 February Ulster Vanguard held its first rally, at Lisburn, attended by some 7,000 people. Its leader, William Craig, who arrived in a car flanked on either side by a uniformed motorcycle escort, said: 'We are determined to preserve our British traditions and way of life. And God help those who get in our way, for we mean business.'

22 February The Official IRA bombed the Officers' Mess of the Parachute Regiment at Aldershot, England, killing 5 female canteen workers, one Catholic padre and a gardener. On the **25th** in Armagh they seriously injured John Taylor, Northern Ireland Minister of State for Home Affairs, in a machine-gun attack.

26 February William Craig, addressing a Vanguard rally at Enniskillen, said: 'We in Vanguard feel the time for talk is over... I can say with confidence we are going to win this struggle. We are going to beat this conspiracy into the ground and we make no accomodation with the enemies of this country, the enemies of democracy.'

February The *UDA Bulletin* published a letter from a woman, which said: 'I have reached the stage where I no longer have any compassion for any nationalist - man, woman or child. After years of destruction, murder, intimidation, I have been driven against my better feelings to the decision - it's them or us. What I want to know is this, where the hell are the MEN in the community? Why have they not started to hit back in the only way these nationalist bastards understand? That is, ruthless, indiscriminate killing.'

4 March A no-warning bomb in the Abercorn Restaurant in central Belfast killed 2 women and injured 130 people, some very seriously. Two sisters who were out shopping for a wedding-dress had both their legs blown off, one of the women - the one getting married - also losing an arm and an eye. The Provisional IRA denied responsibility, but sources later admitted that it was their bomb, but they hadn't left enough time to phone a warning. (2) This month saw the introduction of the 'car bomb' by the Provisionals.

8 March Rev. Ian Paisley said in a statement: 'The Loyalist people can no longer sit idly by and see their country systemically destroyed.'

10 March The Provisional IRA announced a 72-hour truce starting at midnight.

18 March At a Vanguard rally in Ormeau Park, Belfast, attended by over 50,000 people, William Craig said: 'We must build up a dossier of the men and women who are a menace to this country, because if and when the politicians fail us, it may be our job to liquidate the enemy.'

19 March Austin Currie, SDLP, said at an anti-internment rally that there had been the threat of a Protestant backlash for the last fifty years.

20 March A no-warning bomb in Donegall Street, Belfast, killed 6 people. The Provisionals later admitted responsibility, but claimed they gave an adequate warning.

24 March When the British Government's proposal to transfer security from Stormont to Westminster was unacceptable to Brian Faulkner, Direct Rule was imposed by Westminster, and Stormont was 'prorogued'. The Northern Ireland government resigned. William Craig said he intended to make the country ungovernable and thereby force the British government to negotiate with the majority. John Taylor said that the Heath government had acted with treachery towards Northern Ireland. Both wings of the IRA said they would continue with their struggle.

25 March The SDLP called for an immediate cessation of violence, and, addressing the Protestant community, said: 'We recognise that many of you may feel isolated in the present circumstances (but) together a great opportunity awaits us.'

27 March An estimated 190,000 workers supported William Craig's call for a stoppage. In Portadown Vanguard supporters occupied the town and erected barricades. The following day Vanguard held a mass rally of 100,000 at Stormont.

1 April   After the death of a local woman killed in crossfire, women in Andersonstown said they wanted a meeting with Sean MacStiofain, Chief of Staff of the Provisionals, to tell him that the women of the area wanted an end to the violence.

2 April   Sean MacStiofain said that a truce would mean that this generation's fight would be lost.

3 April   A peace meeting in Andersonstown was disrupted by women supporters of the IRA.

4 April   Ruairi O'Bradaigh, President of Provisional Sinn Fein, commenting on Cardinal Conway's statement (on the **2nd**) that the Catholic people wanted an end to the campaign of violence, said there was no evidence to support this. And on the **8th**, Martin McGuinness, for the Provisionals in Derry, said: 'We are fighting on until we get a United Ireland.'

14 April   30 bombs went off throughout the province.

15 April   Joe McCann, the leading Official IRA member in Belfast, was shot dead by troops as he was walking in the Markets area. The imprisoned UVF leader, Gusty Spence, wrote to McCann's widow, saying, 'I salute your husband as an honourable and brave soldier.' Referring to an incident when McCann had ordered the release of two UVF men who had accidentially wandered into the Markets area, he said: 'Joe once did me a good turn indirectly and I never forgot him for his humanity.'

16 April   In Andersonstown 800 women pledged their support for the IRA's campaign.

19 April   The body of a UDR man kidnapped by the IRA was found near Newtownhamilton with explosives strapped to it.

23 April   300 people at a Republican Clubs conference passed a resolution condemning the IRA bombing of civilian targets.

27 April   William Craig said: 'We will only assassinate our enemies as a last desperate resort when we are denied our democratic rights.' A week of rioting in Protestant areas of East Belfast began.

7 May An 'End the Bombing' rally planned by the Republican Club in Ardoyne was called off after threats by Provisionals.

8 May Loyalist and Republican prisoners in the Crumlin Road jail joined forces in their demand for recognition as political prisoners. In one clash with the prison authorities, UVF and Official IRA prisoners were to barricade themselves in a recreation area and hang two flags from the windows, a Republican Tricolour and a white sheet with 'UVF' painted on it. (9)

13 May Following the car bombing of Kelly's Bar in Ballymurphy, Belfast, 4 civilians and 1 solider were killed by gunfire when shooting broke out between Protestant and Catholic gunmen. By the next day the death toll had risen to 8.

14 May In Belfast UDA members set up barricades in Woodvale and warned that unless the 'no-go' areas in the Bogside and Creggan were removed they would set up similar areas in Protestant districts.

15 May After Rev. Ian Paisley had said (on the **12th**) that he was in favour of total integration with the rest of the UK, John Taylor said he would prefer an independent Northern Ireland.

17 May A gunman injured 4 men when he fired into a crowd of Protestant workers leaving Mackie's factory on the Springfield Road, Belfast. A car bomb injured 16 people in the Protestant Donegall Road area. Roy Bradford said that Protestants were feeling betrayed and isolated, and warned that ordinary citizens were being 'inexorably driven into rebellion'.

21 May Rioting in East Belfast erupted after members of the Parachute Regiment stormed newly-erected Protestant barricades.

22 May The day after the Official IRA in Derry had murdered a local man, Ranger William Best, who was on home leave from the British Army, 200 women in the Bogside marched to the Officials' headquarters and demanded they leave the area. The following day they went to see Provisional IRA leaders, and a rally of 1,500 people called for an end to violence.

27 May Several thousand members of the UDA marched to Woodvale Park, Belfast. The UDA now claimed to have an active membership of over 50,000.

28 May 8 people, including 4 IRA members, were killed by an explosion in the Short Strand area of Belfast.

29 May The Official IRA issued a statement saying that, in accordance with the wishes of the people, they had ordered an immediate cessation of hostilities, but reserved the right to self-defensive action. The following day the Provisionals stated that their operations would continue. On **1 June** a mother of 6 from Andersonstown challenged Sean MacStiofain's wife to come and live in a troubled area.

13 June As agitation for a cease-fire intensified (a peace petition circulating West Belfast had 63,000 signatures), Sean MacStiofain in Derry offered to meet with the Secretary of State for Northern Ireland, William Whitelaw, to discuss the Provisionals' peace plan. Mr. Whitelaw rejected this offer, saying he could not respond to 'an ultimatum from terrorists'.

14 June John Hume and Paddy Devlin of the SDLP met with Provisional leaders, who said that before talks could begin, Republican prisoners would have to be granted the status of political prisoners. (2)

15 June John Hume and Paddy Devlin met with the Secretary of State in London. Later the two politicians made a public appeal to the Provisionals for a cease-fire. In Belfast 21 local priests appealed to Mr. Whitelaw to talk to the Provisionals.

20 June A 30-day hunger strike ended in Crumlin Road jail after de facto recognition of political prisoner status was granted to Republican and Loyalist prisoners.

22 June The Provisional IRA said they would suspend operations from midnight on the **26th** (up to that deadline they went on to kill another 6 members of the security forces, and on the 26th itself there were 15 bombings throughout the province). Mr. Whitelaw said that 'Her Majesty's forces will obviously reciprocate'. The following day Seamus Twomey, Belfast Brigade Commander for the Provisional IRA, said it wasn't a cease-fire but a 'bilateral truce' to be observed by both sides.

23 June After 8 Catholics had been assassinated by Protestants during May (and the Provisional Army Council in Dublin had sanctioned the use of retaliation the same month), *Republican News* , the newspaper of the Provisionals, called on Britain to 'control your rabble, for which you and you alone are responsible. It was YOU that bred them; you created them... You cannot and will not pass them off as an Irish problem, they are your problem... KEEP YOUR PROBLEM OFF OUR BACKS. Do you want your boys shot for them or more likely by them? We doubt it, rid yourselves once and for all of their mess.'

27 June On the first day of the truce the Provisionals distributed leaflets in Ballymurphy informing residents that control of law and order in the area now rested with the Provisionals. Under the cease-fire arrangements the Army and the RUC were bound not to enter the 'no-go' areas in Derry and Belfast, and the IRA were able to patrol openly. William Craig said that Loyalists now had no option but to go in and 'clean out the IRA terrorists'.

28 June The Provisional IRA said that as part of their peace proposals (*Eire Nua* - New Ireland) there should be a federal Ireland with four provincial parliaments, including a 9-county Ulster Parliament, Dail Uladh. According to the Provisionals 'Dail Uladh would be representative of Catholic and Protestant, Orange and Green, Left and Right'. 'It would be an Ulster Parliament for the Ulster people. The Unionist oriented people of Ulster would have a working majority within the Province and would therefore have considerable control over their own affairs. That power would be the surest guarantee of their civil and religious liberties within a new Ireland.'

29 June The UDA appealed to the Catholic population to join with Protestants 'and between us work out a new Northern Ireland which will be suitable and admirable for us both'.

3 July Following the UDA's establishment of permanent no-go areas in Belfast, 8,000 masked UDA men confronted the British Army at Ainsworth Avenue.

4 July Two Protestant brothers, aged 19 and 20, who had previously been threatened by UDA members (11), were abducted and murdered on their way to visit a Catholic girl to whom one was engaged. Their mother later said: 'At half past eleven there was a news flash... two bodies had been found and I knew in my heart... I knew it was my two sons... I just couldn't think that my sons were never going to walk into my house again. At times I never want to leave my house because I can walk into their bedrooms and feel near to them. I still say goodnight to them and God bless... I felt like running out into the middle of the road and shouting, "For God's sake stop it - it's senseless".' (10)   At the funeral, attended by many Protestants and Catholics, friends and strangers, the boys' father walked between their coffins, one hand resting on each son all the way to the cemetery.

7 July Six leading Provisionals - Sean MacStiofain, Daithi O'Connaill, Martin McGuinness, Seamus Twomey, Gerry Adams and Ivor Bell - were flown to London for talks with the Secretary of State.

9 July The cease-fire ended when the British Army refused to allow Catholic families to occupy homes in Lenadoon estate, Belfast, which had been vacated by Protestants. The UDA had said it would burn the houses down if they were given to Catholics. The assassinations continued to claim more victims.

10 July Gusty Spence, who had been 'kidnapped' by the UVF while on parole to attend his daughter's wedding, gave a TV interview, in which he said: 'One has only to look at the Shankill Road, the heart of the empire that lies torn and bleeding. We have known squalor. I was born and reared in it. No-one knows better than we do the meaning of slums, the meaning of deprivation, the meaning of suffering for what one believes in, whatever the ideology. In so far as people speak of fifty years of misrule, I wouldn't disagree with that. What I would say is this, that we have suffered every bit as much as the people of the Falls Road, or any other underprivileged quarter, in many cases more so.' (9) Spence was recaptured by troops on **4 November**.

18 July The 100th British soldier to die on active service in the Province since 1969 was killed in Belfast. (He was an only son, and a few weeks later his father, who had talked of 'joining him', hanged himself in the loft of their home.) In London, members of the Provisional IRA met Harold Wilson, leader of the British Labour Party.

21 July 'Bloody Friday'. 22 bombs went off in Belfast killing 9 people and injuring 130. Because many of the bodies had been dismembered it was at first thought that more people had been killed. When the media described the bits of bodies being collected in polythene bags the province was horrified. The Provisionals accepted responsibility, but said they had given adequate warnings. An ex-Provisional, Maria Maguire, was later to write: 'All along we had known that there were risks of civilian casualties due to misunderstandings of our warnings and delays in acting on them. I could not

38

avoid the conclusion that the probability of civilian casualties had been accepted, perhaps even planned.' (12) The Executive of the Republican Clubs called on Provisional members to dissociate themselves from the leadership. One of those who died was the 14-year-old son, an only child, of Rev. Joseph Parker, who later said: 'When I got to the mortuary I knew there was a boy, the body of a boy there. I looked immediately for someone with fair hair. I was somewhat relieved that the hair was dark, but, of course, it was singed and burnt dark with the heat of the explosion. I thought immediately, though: it's not Stephen. And then I looked again. I recognised the shirt as similar to the one Stephen had been wearing, but again it had been affected by the explosion. The belt was a Scout belt: he was a Scout, and a few days before he had put those studs all round the belt and stood there getting me to admire them. I asked one of the men to look in the pockets, I wanted to be sure. Anyway, he looked in the pockets and found this box of matches - trick matches that Stephen had used that evening before to fool me... Then I knew it was Stephen.' (10)

31 July In 'Operation Motorman' the British Army moved into the Bogside in Derry to end the 'no-go' area. No resistance was offered, as the Provisional IRA had withdrawn to avoid an open confrontation with the large Army forces. In the village of Claudy no-warning car bombs killed 6 people (3 more were to die later). 80 people were killed this month in the violence, and as 36 of them were civilian assassinations 'feelings in the Catholic community had reached something approaching hysteria' (11), especially after false rumours circulated that a female victim had been tortured and mutilated.

19 August 5,000 UDA men marched in companies to a rally in East Belfast. The SDLP blamed the UDA for the recent spate of sectarian, and often extremely brutal, murders (one victim had been stabbed 150 times).

23 August The UDA accused Ulster Vanguard of failing to carry out any of its threats.

10 September After nights of violence between Protestants and the Army, in which 2 men were shot dead by troops, NICRA said it supported the UDA's demand that the Paras be withdrawn from the Shankill area of Belfast.

16 September 7,000 UDA men, many wearing masks and combat jackets, marched through Belfast city centre.

19 September In an interview with the *Belfast Telegraph*, the Chairman of the UDA, Jim Anderson, said: 'I feel that people are beginning to catch on about the Unionist government. The ordinary man is starting to think for himself about the fifty years of misrule that he did have. If a Unionist candidate came down a street, all he had to do was wave a flag and beat a drum and he was elected for the next five years, and you didn't see him for the next five years. People are starting to catch on. People are starting to know.'

21 September Outside Belfast City Hall, Rev. Joseph Parker, whose son Stephen was killed on 'Bloody Friday', began a protest fast to express his frustration at all those who were failing to tackle the problems of violence. He said: 'The killing goes on and on. When will it end? I feel that it is my duty.' The following day he was joined by a Catholic girl student.

24 September The mother of a policeman who had been seriously injured in an ambush near the border collapsed and died at her son's bedside in Newry hospital.

25 September The SDLP refused to take part in the Darlington conference in County Durham, England, called to discuss the future of Northern Ireland.

30 September What was described as the largest show of Protestant strength since the signing of the Covenant 60 years before, took place when an estimated 100,000 Loyalists (including 20,000 UDA members) attended a rally at Stormont.

16 October After 2 men were killed by Army vehicles during rioting in East Belfast, a UDA leader was reported to have said: 'To hell with the British Army. The British government and the British Army are now our enemies.' The next day Protestant gunmen attacked the Army in different parts of Belfast.

19 October William Craig said: 'Let us put bluff aside. I am prepared to kill and those behind me have my full support. We will not surrender.'

30 October The British Government's Green Paper on the future of Northern Ireland talked of the need for an 'Irish Demension' - John Hume, SDLP, applauded this as the 'first glimmerings of reality that Northern problems should be faced in an Irish context'.

2 November Billy Hull, spokesman for the Loyalist Association of Workers (LAW), told a rally that the middle-class Unionist politicians 'who are now looking around to see where they will go', will never again 'represent the Loyalist working class of this country'.

16 November The British Prime Minister, Edward Heath, warned against the talk of UDI, saying that a bloodbath would ensue, and that Britain would withdraw its subsidy. Two days later a UDA spokeman said that they would accept this 'rather than be threatened or bullied by you'.

20 November Ballymurphy priest Father Desmond Wilson read a statement signed by 65 priests accusing the British Army of harassing and subjecting Catholic civilians to degrading treatment, and shooting unarmed people.

28 November In the Republic, Sean MacStiofain, who had been charged with IRA membership and had gone on a hunger and thirst strike, went on to fluids after the intervention of Father Sean McManus.

3 December The Offences against the State Act came into force in the Republic.

6 December The Secretary of State for Northern Ireland, William Whitelaw, announced the formation of a new 'murder squad' to deal with the sectarian assassinations which had continued unabated - 70 Catholics and 36 Protestants had been murdered so far this year.

7 December Senior UDA officer Ernest Elliott was found murdered in a van in Belfast. It was said that Elliott had expressed left-wing views and had engaged in secret discussions with representatives of the Official IRA. (11) Loyalists were suspected of the killing.

9 December John Taylor said that Loyalists should consider the merits of negotiated independence for Northern Ireland.

17 December On BBC radio William Craig said of sectarian murders: 'I personally am not happy about what is happening but if it is impossible to win our democratic rights without this sort of thing happening then I am prepared to tolerate it.'

20 December 5 men were killed in a Loyalist machine-gun attack on a Catholic bar in Derry. The group of peace women in the Bogside in Derry said: 'Every mother, every wife, every sweetheart, must realise guns kill and must be done away with as a means of settling anything. The anguish and grief of the families is a blot on our consciences.' The report of the Diplock Commission recommended trial without a jury as a way to combat terrorism.

30 December A letter to the *Belfast Telegraph*, appealing for peace, said: 'We want to know that men can walk from the Falls to the Shankill and from Woodvale to Ballymurphy without the slightest fear. We want to know that the children of Andersonstown can meet the children of Sandy Row and enjoy the things that normal children enjoy the world over.'

31 December A man flagged down a bus on the Springfield Road in Belfast, then fired into it wounding four people, before escaping into the Protestant Highfield estate.

The death toll for the year: 103 Army, 41 RUC & UDR and 323 civilians (of whom 121 were classified as assassinations: 81 catholics and 40 Protestants). This was to be the worst death toll in the twenty years.

1973

1 January In the Republic, a young engaged couple were found murdered in County Donegal near the border. A UDA member was later sought by the Gardai. Great Britain and Ireland officially joined the European Economic Community.

3 January In a joint statement, the leaders of the 4 main churches in Ulster said: 'We appeal to the whole community to root out this evil - tell the murderers and assassins they are on their own. The horror of recent assassinations haunts our minds. We are conscious of the multiplying numbers of women and children who are being robbed of the men they love and who are nightly in fear. These sectarian and political murders, whether of civilians or security personnel, have brought shame to our land and tragedy to countless homes. They are a crime before God and are a disgrace to our common Christian heritage.'

4 January Tommy Herron, Vice-Chairman of the UDA, in a statement warned all those involved in sectarian assassinations to stop forthwith. The following day the Inner Council of the UDA backed Herron, saying: 'We wish to make it quite clear to all those involved in these murders to stop now or face the wrath of the UDA.'

13/14 January In what was described as 'Northern Ireland's blackest week-end of violence for several months', 3 policemen died and 3 others were injured in a spate of bombings and shootings.

15 January The Provisional IRA said that Sean MacStiofain had been ordered to come off his hunger-strike. When he was eventually released from prison he was removed from his position as Chief-of-Staff.

28 January Ex-UDA leader, Dave Fogel, who had departed Belfast suddenly with his family, in an interview with the *Sunday Times* revealed that there was a power struggle going on within the UDA: 'We are mixing with dangerous and evil men out for their own gains and not for the interests of the ordinary working-class Protestant people of Ulster.' He said that he hoped the two working class communities could eventually unite.

30 January Following 5 murders within 48 hours (4 Catholics and 1 Protestant), Tommy Herron said that as the Provisional IRA had just continued with its campaign of bombing and killing in the period he had called off the assassins, the UDA could no longer try to restrain Protestant extremists. The following day the Provisionals threatened 'ruthless retaliatory action against the UDA to end sectarian assassinations'.

2 February Sinn Fein (Official) said that the Provisionals' declaration of war on the UDA was a desperate attempt to push Protestants and Catholics into confrontation.

3 February Six men, including 4 Provisional IRA volunteers, died in shooting incidents in the New Lodge area of Belfast. The Army claimed to have shot them during a gun battle, but local people said 2 were shot from a passing car believed to contain Protestant extremists. The weekend's violence, with 13 dead (8 of whom were assassination victims), left the province in a high state of tension and shock.

7 February Belfast experienced a total blackout of electricity during a one-day strike called by the United Loyalist Council. The strike was called after the first Protestants were detained under the Detention of Terrorists Order. In the widespread violence that accompanied the strike 5 people died, including a member of the Fire Service killed by a Loyalist gunman as he tried to put out a fire.

12 February William Craig, speaking at Vanguard's first anniversary rally, after claiming that the divisive factor in Ulster was 'not how you worship God, but the different national loyalties', asked: 'could we not all owe allegiance to Ulster... a dominion of Ulster must not be... something for the Protestants as such to control... Perhaps we should be considering checks and restraints.' He received a standing ovation. Following the speech Brian Faulkner said he could no longer consider Mr. Craig as a member of the Unionist Party, for any kind of independence was contrary to Unionism.

6 March Talks took place between Paddy Devlin and Ivan Cooper of the SDLP, and William Craig and John Taylor. The UDA said that Craig had their full confidence. On the **11th**, in an RTE interview, William Craig spoke of the 'common ground' he believed existed, and the feeling that 'the future will be decided only by the people of Northern Ireland'.

8 March In England, one person died and 180 were injured after two bombs in London, claimed the next day by the Provisional IRA. 7 men and 3 women, including the Price sisters, were charged with the bombing on the **12th** and convicted on **15 November**. The Border Poll was held in Northern Ireland - it found 57% of the electorate in favour of Union with Great Britain.

20 March The British Government issued its White Paper, with a proposal for an Assembly elected by proportional representation, and provision for a Council of Ireland. Nationalist political groups gave the paper a cautious welcome.

23 March Girls lured 4 soldiers to a house on the Antrim Road, Belfast, where IRA gunmen murdered 3 of them and seriously injured the fourth.

29 March The British Prime Minister, Edward Heath, said on TV, with regard to Ulster Loyalists who would not abide by the law: 'There are no more disloyal people in the United Kingdom than people who take that attitude. They are, in fact, disloyalists.'

44

20 May As the killings and bombings continued, Canon Padraig Murphy said: 'We have all had enough. We earnestly ask those whose hands are stained with blood to reconsider the path down which they are trying to force us - the price they are asking us to pay.'

9 June An internal upheaval within the UDA led to the removal of 4 company commanders and 18 senior officers. Younger and more militant members were reported to have taken control. There had also been continuing expressions of anger at the increase in corruption and extortion carried out by UDA members. Following a bomb attack on a Catholic pub a caller to a local newspaper used the name 'Ulster Freedom Fighters' (UFF) for the first time; they later claimed they were a breakaway group from the UDA. Up to now, no Protestant body had ever admitted killing Catholics.

12 June 6 people were killed and 18 very seriously injured by a car bomb in Coleraine.

15 June The brother-in-law of former Vice-Chairman of the UDA Tommy Herron, was shot dead at Mr. Herron's home. Mr. Herron accused the Provisional IRA of attempting to murder him, but Loyalists were strongly suspected.

30 June The Northern Ireland Assembly elections took place.

2 July Liam Cosgrave, Taoiseach of the Irish Republic, said that if a United Ireland were to come about now it would only 'dangerously exacerabate tensions and fears (and) double the problem at a stroke'.

3 August The Littlejohn brothers, at their trial for armed robbery in the Irish Republic, claimed they had been engaged in undercover work for the British Ministry of Defence.

16 September Tommy Herron was found murdered in Belfast. Widespread feeling that Loyalists were responsible.

23 September Mother Theresa of Calcutta suddenly announced that she was pulling her welfare mission out of West Belfast. Her four Asian Missionary Sisters of Charity had organised numerous community projects and activities - a children's creche, a choir, and classes in music, woodwork, leather craft, painting, dress-making and drama. Local people felt that the nuns wouldn't have left these projects unfinished unless they had been ordered to depart by the Church. An attempt to seek an explanation from the Church authorities didn't receive a satisfactory response. Father Desmond Wilson claimed that some clergy 'believed it unseemly that missionary sisters should come here from India or anywhere else'. (13)

9 November Cardinal Conway asked why official condemnation of assassinations of Catholics was 'so muted'.

17 November The UVF in a statement said they would call a 43-day cease-fire from midnight on the **18th**. On **24 December** they announced that it had been indefinitely extended.

21 November After talks between the Secretary of State and Unionist, SDLP and Alliance Assembly members at Stormont, an agreement to form an Executive was announced. Rev. William Beattie, DUP, called it ' the greatest betrayal since Lundy'.

22 November Liam Cosgrave, Taoiseach of the Irish Republic, said: 'We are on the road to peace now.' The Provisional IRA said they would destroy the Executive just as they had destroyed the old Stormont.

1 December Gerry Fitt at the SDLP conference in Belfast said he had never felt such hope for the future.

5 December Fighting broke out during a debate at the Assembly when Unionist members were attacked by DUP and Vanguard members.

6 December The British Prime Minster, Edward Heath, opened the talks at Sunningdale, Berkshire, by welcoming the Taoiseach of the Irish Republic and members of the new Executive. He said he also welcomed the opportunity to discuss the structure of a Council of Ireland. The 4 days of talks were to result in the 'Sunningdale Agreement'. At the Ulster Hall, Belfast, 600 delegates from Unionist Party constituency associations, Vanguard, DUP and the Orange Order, voted to form a new United Ulster Unionist Council (UUUC) to provide common leadership.

9 December Brian Faulkner, Chief Executive designate, said: 'I believe the agreement heralds a new dawn not just for Northern Ireland but for the whole of Ireland.'

10 December   A new Ulster Army Council, mainly composed of Loyalist paramilitary organisations, said they would oppose any moves towards a Council of Ireland.

31 December   At the new Executive's first meeting a hope was expressed that 1974 would be the 'Year of Reconciliation'.

Death Toll for the year: 171 civilians, 58 Army, 22 RUC and UDR.

1974

1 January   The Northern Ireland Executive officially took up duty.   The Provisional IRA in its New Year message said: 'We look forward with confidence to 1974 as a year in which the British rule in Ireland shall be destroyed and the curse of alien power banished from our land for all time.'

4 January   The UDA said that traditional Unionism was dead and Loyalists now had to shape their own destiny.

6 January   Desmond Boal, former DUP Chairman, said he would now consider a federal Irish Parliament, together with a provincial Ulster Parliament. Rev. Ian Paisley and William Craig dissociated themselves from Boal's views. On the **8th** Ruairi O'Bradaigh, President of Provisional Sinn Fein, said that the proposal was 'approximately' what Sinn Fein had been proposing. On the **12th** the UVF praised Boal's 'courage and honesty'. On the **17th** Boal met with Frank McManus, Unity MP, for informal talks.

7 January   After the Ulster Unionist Council (on the **4th**) had rejected the Council of Ireland proposed in the Sunningdale Agreement, Brian Faulkner resigned as Unionist Party leader.   On the **22nd** Harry West was elected 'Official' Unionist Party (OUP) leader. On **4 February** a pro-Assembly Unionist group was set up to support Brian Faulkner.

13 January   Rev. Ian Paisley, on a radio programme, said: 'I am convinced that the British government does not want us. I am absolutely sure.'

24 January   Brian Faulkner said: 'Virtually every one of judgement now agrees that it has been a great source of weakness and instability to Northern Ireland over half a century that its Roman Catholic community, representing one third of the population, has not played a commensurate part in the life and affairs of the province.'

January Dr. Ian Adamson published *The Cruthin*, in which he pointed out that both communities in the North of Ireland shared a common heritage that was far more ancient than they realised, a heritage that not only pre-dated the 'Plantation', but reached back in history long before the arrival of the Celts.

1 February Liam Cosgrove, Taoiseach of the Irish Republic, and 7 of his ministers flew by helicopter to Hillsborough, County Down, for a meeting with Northern Ireland Assembly members.

3 February The UVF, who on **29 January** had appealed for an end to sectarian assassinations, now called for peace and reconciliation. Maire Drumm, Vice President of Provisional Sinn Fein, welcomed the gesture. On the **21st** the *Times* revealed that members of the UVF Brigade Staff had met Cathal Goulding, Chief of Staff of the Official IRA. On **30 June** the *Observer* claimed that the UVF had also met with the Provisionals in February. On **1 April** one of the UVF leaders who took part in the talks with the Officials was shot dead in his car on the Shankill Road.

4 February The IRA exploded a bomb on a coach carrying army personnel on the M4 motorway in England. 8 soldiers and one woman with her 2 children were all killed.

15 February A statement issued by a group calling itself the Ulster Citizen Army threatened to kill business executives if the Government succeeded in throwing Northern Ireland into 'vicious sectarian warfare'.

22 February The NI Community Relations Commission stated that 60,000 people had been forced to flee from their homes during the past 4 years.

28 February The UK General Election, in which the British Labour Party defeated the Conservatives, led to the UUUC winning 11 out of the 12 Northern Ireland seats. The total vote for anti-Sunningdale candidates was 59%.

2 March In *Republican News*, the Provisional IRA called on parents to 'instill more discipline into their children', saying that vandalism and crime only brought Irishmen 'down to the degrading level that the British have achieved'.

22 March The Ulster Workers' Council (UWC) said that should Westminster policies be imposed on the Ulster people 'grave industrial consequences will ensue'. The UWC included former members of LAW, representatives from Loyalist paramilitary groups, and politicians who were co-opted onto the executive committee.

24 March The *Sunday Telegraph* reported that a 'no-conflict policy' had been agreed between Republican and Loyalist prisoners. In an article in a community magazine (*The Third Force*, **April 1986**), UVF leader Gusty Spence later said: 'The paramilitary representatives attempted to 'export' this co-operation to the outside world through the medium of a 'downtown' office, wherein welfare groups interested in paramilitary prisoners could meet and maximise their welfare efforts, and Heaven knows where such co-operation could have led Northern Ireland!' Spence claimed that 'devious and unenlightened publicity', 'petty' sectarian attitudes from local politicians, and deliberate government obstruction, destroyed what he described as 'an important breakthrough'.

26 March John Hume, SDLP deputy leader, when asked on RTE if he thought Sunningdale would lead to a United Ireland, replied that he hoped it would, but by agreement. Paddy Devlin was later to say that the SDLP's aim at Sunningdale had been to establish all-Ireland institutions which would 'produce the dymanic that could lead ultimately to an agreed single State for Ireland'. (14)

31 March The Republican Clubs spokesman condemned the escalating bombing campaign by the Provisional IRA, and said people were now accepting the bombing as the order of the day.

3 April Austin Currie, SDLP, one of those involved in launching a rent and rates strike against Internment in August 1971, now, as Minster for Housing in the new Executive, said that all arrears must be paid in full, and non-payers would be levied 25p per week and could have payments deducted from their Social Security Benefits.

4 April The Secretary of State, Merlyn Rees, speaking in the House of

Commons, said he proposed to remove Sinn Fein and the UVF from the list of proscribed organisations. (On **16 February** the former Secretary of State, Francis Pym, had invited the two organisations to advance their views 'through the democratic process'.)

11 April A total of 308,410 Loyalists had now signed a petition against the Sunningdale Agreement.

30 April After the Minister of Education in the Executive had outlined proposals for the integrated education of Protestant and Catholic schoolchildren, Canon Padraig Murphy, Parish priest in the Falls Road district, said the scheme was 'naive and ill-informed'.

10 May The Ulster Workers' Council said that the recent Westminster election had removed the mandate from the Executive, and new elections should be called. If this was not done, and the Northern Ireland Assembly endorsed the Sunningdale Agreement, they threatened to embark on a 'full-scale constitutional stoppage' throughout the province.

14 May A few hours after the Assembly had endorsed the Sunningdale Agreement, Harry Murray, spokesman for the UWC, informed journalists that the strike was now on, saying: 'It is a grave responsibility, but it is not ours. It is Brian Faulkner's.'

15 May As the province felt the first effects of the strike, Rev. William Beattie, DUP deputy leader, said: 'The pressure will be built up on Dublin and London until the whole system breaks completely and we get victory.' Brian Faulkner in a statement about the strikers asked: 'Where do they come from? Who elected them? What is their authority?'

16 May Road-blocks and barricades were set up in various parts of Belfast by UDA members wearing combat clothing and dark glasses. The UWC published a list of what it considered to be 'essential services'.

17 May No-warning car bombs exploded in Dublin and Monaghan killing 27 people (5 more were to die later) and injuring over 100. Three girls were among the Dublin victims, one of whom was decapitated, the bodies of the other two fused together by the heat of the blast. Loyalists were believed responsible for the bombs. UDA Press Officer, Sammy Smyth, said: 'I am very happy about the bombing. There is a war with the Free State and now we are laughing at them.' A Loyalist politician is reported to have said: 'Slap it into you fellahs - you've deserved every bit of it.' (15)

18 May   There were long queues outside bakeries and greengrocers' shops. After the Secretary of State, Merlyn Rees, had met with members of the Executive and said that there could be no negotiations under duress, the UWC called for an all-out stoppage from midnight on the **19th.**

19 May   As electricity supplies all over the province dwindled, the Secretary of State declared a State of Emergency to protect all essential services.

20 May   The UWC said that apart from the supply of bread and milk, and the opening of food shops and post offices between 2 and 6pm, all other industries and services were requested to support the stoppage. Cecil Parker, Conservative MP, said that the UWC was far more representative of Ulster workers than many of the organisations with which the Government had previously negotiated.

21 May   A group of 200 people, led by the General Secretary of the British Trade Union Congress, Len Murray, and protected by British troops, tried to stage a 'back to work' march to Belfast Shipyard. An angry crowd pelted them with rotten vegetables.

24 May   After passes had been given out at UWC headquarters, men in paramilitary uniform checked the credentials of motorists queuing at 'approved' petrol stations. Harry Murray of the UWC had dispatched the first petrol tanker to the Falls Road in Belfast, a gesture which impressed the IRA's Chief-of-Staff, Daithi O'Connaill. (15) A statement following talks at Chequers between the British Prime Minister Harold Wilson, and leaders of the Northern Ireland Executive, affirmed that the Executive provided the only basis of peace and good government in Northern Ireland. Harry Murray said: 'We are going to stick it out right to the end. It's no surrender. Ulster is not for sale.' The *Irish Times* said: 'The Labour lads on the other side of the water are no match for the corner-boys of Belfast; those who held hands and sang The Red Flag at the end of their party conference have been routed by genuine proletarians.'

25 May   Hundreds of farmers blocked roads throughout the province with tractors to demonstrate their support for the strike. On national TV the Prime Minister, Harold Wilson, said that the people of Ulster spent their lives 'sponging' on Westminster.

26 May People in the streets of Belfast wore sponges in their lapels in derision at Harold Wilson's speech, and the UDA said his allegation was contemptible. Political leaders of all shades over the next few days were to agree that the speech was regrettable and counter-productive. Maire Drumm, Vice-President of Sinn Fein, said she knew how the Protestants felt: 'It made me sick to hear an Englishman saying those things about Irishmen.' (15) SDLP members of the Executive said that the British Government's inability to act against the strikers made them feel so badly let down the Executive was on the point of collapse.

27 May Secretary of State, Merlyn Rees, ordered British troops to occupy the British Petroleum refinery and take over the distribution of petrol to essential users. In retaliation the UWC called for a complete withdrawal by all workers from all industries. In London a Downing Street spokesman said that the Prime Minister was keeping in constant touch with events from his holiday in the Scilly Islands. Most areas of the province experienced a total blackout of electricity. Harry Murray, for the UWC, said: 'We can take it as far as we need to, and further. We will break this regime up at Stormont.'

28 May The Northern Ireland Executive collapsed. The Chief Executive, Brian Faulkner, read a statement which said: 'The degree of consent needed to sustain the Executive does not at present exist.' In the evening thousands of people in Protestant areas celebrated around bonfires.

29 May The UWC recommended a phased return to work. The Prime Minister, Harold Wilson, said on TV: 'This is a totally unconstitutional thing which we have never met before in any part of the United Kingdom. (It) is a singularly un-British way of going on.'

30 May The NI Chamber of Commerce and Industry estimated that the strike had cost the province £30m. Neil Kinnock, Labour MP, said that British trade unionists viewed the divisions and destruction in Ulster with disbelief, and he recommended: 'Leave them to stew in their own juice.'

3 June Tam Dalyell, Labour MP, reporting on 4 hours of talks with the UWC, said he got the impression that the UWC had their lines of communication with the extremists on 'the other side'. He expressed amazement that, considering what they said about each other, they still seemed able to get on

52

together, and added: 'The Irish have a peculiarly Irish way of doing things.'

13 June The Taoiseach, Liam Cosgrave, said that people in the South were having less and less desire for unity with a people so deeply imbued with violence.

25 June Rev. Mark Tierney, a senior history master from Limerick, writing in *Oideas,* said that some of the responsibility for the distrust and hatred in Northern Ireland could be placed on the shoulders of history teachers and text-book authors. Local historian Ian Adamson later claimed that Ulster people were taught either an 'English' history or an 'Irish' history, and rarely a history that revealed what both communities in the North had in common. He said that Ulster had an extremely rich historical and cultural heritage which, if properly explored, could contribute positively to helping the two communities rediscover their shared identity. (16)

4 July Merlyn Rees said that a new Northern Ireland Bill would make the Secretary of State responsible for government in the province. The Bill would provide for a Constitutional Convention to be elected, which would be asked to prepare a report. This report would only be acceptable to the UK government if it was also found to be acceptable to a broad section of opinion in Northern Ireland.

9 July Harry Murray, who resigned from the UWC following criticism of his attendance at an Oxford seminar organised by the British Irish Organisation, described Loyalist politicians as 'cowboys' who would 'argue to doomsday while the people in the street go on suffering'. The next day the UDA said it supported Mr. Murray, and claimed he had been sacrificed for dubious reasons.

17 July A woman was killed and 36 people injured, many seriously, by a no-warning bomb in the Tower of London.

20 July The UDA, who had provided the backbone and 'muscle' behind the May strike, resigned from the UWC. The following day, the UDA's Chairman, Andy Tyrie, said: 'We have done some awful things during our war effort because we felt it was justified at the time, but we feel we can sort things out now by getting Protestant and Catholics together.' He invited representatives of the Catholic community to take part in talks. On **1 August** discussions took place between the SDLP and the UDA.

53

7 August Paddy Doherty of the Bogside Community Association said that the UWC strike was 'brilliantly conceived and executed... Britain does not need Ulster Loyalists but Ireland does'.

18 August 19 Provisional IRA prisoners escaped from Portlaoise prison in the Republic, after blasting their way outside.

5 September Harry Murray, former Chairman of the UWC, said: 'We will have to come together as one community or we will perish together.'

6 September Garrett FitzGerald, Irish Minister for Foreign Affairs, said that the decline of the Protestant population in the Irish Republic as a result of the Catholic Church's policy towards mixed marriages had intensified Northern Protestant fears. He asked whether the 'inter-community strife in Northern Ireland derives from the fact that the two sections of the community ... have largely retained their cultural identities because of the religious barrier to inter-marriage'.

23 September A British Army magazine stated that so far this year 70 Catholics and 30 Protestants had been 'knee-capped' in punishment shootings.

5 October In England, 5 people were killed and 54 injured when no-warning bombs exploded at two pubs in Guildford, Surrey.

11 October In the UK General Election, the UUUC won 10 out of the 12 Westminster seats. The UVF fielded a candidate under the banner of the Volunteer Political Party, with mildly socialist policies. Loyalist politicians, Orangemen and religious fundamentalists 'waged a campaign against the VPP which featured allegations of Communism, atheism, pro-Republicanism, debauchery and all manner of vices.' (17) Glen Barr was suspended from the UUUC after campaigning for the VPP's candidate, who received 2,600 votes.

14 October As assassinations continued to horrify the province, a caller to a local newspaper, claiming to represent the Ulster Protestant Action Force, warned that the killing of Catholics would continue until the Provisional IRA was eradicated. The *Times* reported that UDA officers had been trying to find a way out of the assassination campaign.

15 October Republican prisoners at Long Kesh set fire to huts in their

54

compounds. A pitched battle took place with the security forces, and 300 of the prisoners managed to take shelter in the loyalist compounds, until a Loyalist leader, John McKeague, negotiated a safe passage for them with the authorities. On the **27th** it was revealed that the Provisional IRA Commander in the prison had written to the UDA Commander apologising for any suffering caused to Loyalists as a result of the riot.

27 October Rev. Joseph Parker, whose son Stephen had died on 'Bloody Friday', announced that he and his wife were emigrating to Canada. Some months before he had founded the 'Witness for Peace' movement, but he claimed his colleagues had not invited him to preach in their churches, and he had no choice but to start a new life elsewhere. He said: 'I am extremely disappointed at how things have gone for me. I am a very sad man, a very lonely man, and I am amazed at the attitude of some of our clergy to the present situation. I am leaving my country and my church because I have been completely ostracised.'

14 November Both the UDA and Provisional Sinn Fein confirmed that they had held separate talks with Lybian leaders.

17 November On an ITV programme Daithi O'Connaill, Chief of Staff of the Provisionals, said, when referring to the bombing campaign in Britain, that 'we strike at economic, military, political and judicial targets', and although the IRA had no quarrel with the 'ordinary British people', the time had come when they must suffer the consequences of the war being waged in their name in Ireland. On the **19th** Sammy Smyth of the UDA said his first reaction to the interview was one of 'sheer unadulterated hatred'. 'At that moment I could have, without a twinge of compassion, bombed every well-filled chapel in Belfast... They had nurtured this serpent, this reptile, that dared on the programme to call himself human.'

21 November In England 19 people were killed and 182 injured by IRA bombs at two public houses in Birmingham. 5 men from Northern Ireland living in Birmingham were arrested boarding the Heysham-Belfast ferry. They were later charged with the murders, but on **1 December** the IRA denied that any of those arrested were members of their organisation.

25 November As the killings continued the Chief Constable of the RUC, James Flanagan appealed 'to the people of Northern Ireland to come forward as never before and give us their maximum help'.

29 November The Prevention of Terrorism Bill became law.

3 December A survey by the NI Housing Executive revealed that almost 20% of the province's houses were 'statutorily unfit', most of them concentrated in the Shankill and Falls areas of Belfast and in County Fermanagh. 91% lacked at least 4 of the 5 basic amenities: a bath, inside toilet, wash hand basin, kitchen sink, and cold water at three points.

8 December The Irish Republican Socialist Party (IRSP) was formed by breakaway elements from Official Sinn Fein.

10 December A delegation of Protestant clergymen met representatives of the Provisionals at Feakle, in the Irish Republic, for peace talks.

12 December The DUP Executive in a statement said: 'Are these men so naive as to believe that their voices of sweet reasonableness will dissuade Satan's agents of death and destruction from continuing their evil campaign?'

20 December After the Provisional IRA Army Council had voted 5-2 for a temporary cease-fire (the two Northern representatives opposing it) (2), the Provisionals announced they would suspend operations over an 11-day period between **22nd December** and **2 January**. The decison, the statement said, was prompted by the courageous and positive action of the Church representatives.

31 December The Secretary of State, Merlyn Rees, said that 'if a genuine and sustained cessation of violence' occurred the government 'would not be found wanting in its response'.

Death toll for the year: 165 civilians, 30 Army, and 22 RUC & UDR

1975

2 January The Provisional IRA announced they would extend their Christmas cease-fire by 14 days.

3 January The UDA warned that if there was any retreat on the part of the British government in response to the cease-fire (which the UDA felt was just a tactic by the Provisionals to allow reorganisation), then there could be an escalation of violence not previously experienced.

6 January The West Belfast Brigade of the UDA, under the leadership of Charles Harding Smith, split from the Inner Council which was led by Andy Tyrie. On the **14th** Harding Smith was injured by a gunman, and a second attempt to assassinate him was made on **6 February**.

19 January Peace marches in Belfast and Dublin attracted between 10,000 and 20,000 people. On the **26th** 10,000 gathered in Derry and 3,000 in Newry.

30 January The Gardiner Committee report expressed criticism of 'special category status' for terrorist prisoners.

5 February In the House of Commons Merlyn Rees said that if the IRA ended all offensive operations the Army would be slowly reduced to peacetime levels and ultimately withdrawn to barracks, there would be no more interim custody orders and internment would be phased out, and there would be no action by the security forces which could be interpreted as harassment by the civilian population.

9 February The Provisional Army Council announced that 'hostilities against the Crown forces' would be suspended from **10 February**.

11 February The Secretary of State, Merlyn Rees, announced that 'incident centres' were to be set up in various parts of the province, where contact between Provisional Sinn Fein and Northern Ireland Office (NIO) officials could take place. Both the SDLP and Unionists were to express concern over the status this gave to the Provisional IRA.

20 February The chairman of the recently formed IRSP was murdered by the Official IRA. A bitter Republican feud was to develop in which the Belfast leader of the Official IRA was killed on **28 April**.

24 February The Secretary of State said that 80 detainees would be freed in the coming weeks, and if he was satisfied that the violence had come to a permanent end, he would consider eventually ending detention without trial.

26 February The UDA said it would set up its own vigilante policing system

57

in Loyalist areas, unless normal policing was resumed in Republican areas.

15 March When two UDA men were murdered in a bar in the York Road area of Belfast, it heralded a period of feuding between the UDA and the UVF.

18 March The Price sisters, sentenced for their part in the London bombings of March 1973, were transferred to Armagh prison from England. The sisters had gone on a hunger strike lasting 206 days (for 167 of which they had been force-fed) demanding such a transfer, but had come off it on **8 June 1974** after Home Secretary Roy Jenkins said he believed such a move would be possible, but he would not make any decision under intimidation. On **30 April 1980** Marion Price was released from prison, when her life was considered in danger from anorexia nervosa, and on **22 April 1981** Delores Price was released because of the same condition.

5 April In Belfast 2 people were killed when a bomb was thrown into a Catholic bar in the New Lodge area. A few hours later a bomb was thrown into the Mountainview Tavern on the Shankill Road, killing 5 Protestants.

29 April As the sectarian assassinations and internal feuding continued to claim more lives, the Secretary of State Merlyn Rees warned that if the horrifying level of violence went unchecked rational political debate could become impossible.

1 May In the Northern Ireland Convention elections the 46 elected UUUC members had a substantial majority over the combined opposition.

26 May Rev. William Arlow, one of the clergymen involved in the cease-fire negotiations, claimed that the Government had given a firm commitment to the IRA that British troops would withdraw from Ulster if the Convention broke down. The Government denied this.

28 May UDA leader Andy Tyrie said that Loyalist paramilitary groups were preparing for a doomsday situation in the event of a British withdrawal.

16 June At Westminster the Secretary of State, Merlyn Rees, said that the cease-fire had brought into focus the violence within and between the two communities. Father Desmond Wilson, who had initiated numerous self-help projects aimed at tackling the unemployment and alienation he found in Ballymurphy estate, announced his resignation from his Diocese

58

following disagreements with the Catholic hierarchy. On the **19th** 1,000 people attended a meeting in his support, and the following day it was announced that a European trust fund would provide him with finances to let him continue his community work. Father Wilson's own house in Ballymurphy (Springhill Community House) was used as a base for numerous community projects and discussion groups.

31 July 3 members of the Miami Showband were murdered by the UVF near Newry; 2 UVF members blew themselves up as they were planting a bomb in the showband's van.

13 August 5 people were killed and 40 injured in an IRA bomb attack on the Bayardo Bar on the Shankill Road, Belfast.

15 August A car bomb in a side street near Divis Flats injured 35 people and damaged a large number of houses. Later in the same area a Protestant council worker delivering emergency supplies of hardboard to residents was dragged from his lorry by an angry crowd and shot dead.

17 August The Roman Catholic Primate of Ireland, Cardinal Conway, issued a statement expressing his horror at recent murders. A message from the priests and people of the Falls Road was read at services at the Protestant Shankill Mission deploring the death of the council worker and expressing shame that those who murdered him came from the Catholic community. A large number of Catholics attended his funeral on the **19th**.

August There were reports that some members of the Provisional IRA, unhappy with the cease-fire, were defecting to the new Irish National Liberation Army (INLA, the armed wing of the IRSP) which began to operate in **July**.

1 September Four Orangemen were killed when gunmen, who later claimed to be from the South Armagh Republican Action Force, burst into an Orange Hall at Newtownhamilton. The bodies of two missing men were found in Belfast, believed to be victims of the UVF/UDA feud.

10 September The UDA announced its support for William Craig after he had resigned as leader of the Vanguard Convention Party in protest at the UUUC's decision to calls off talks with the SDLP. On the **26th** he said that it would be madness as well as unjust and dishonest to exclude the SDLP from a voluntary coalition.

23 September After 18 bombs had gone off throughout the province the IRA in Dublin denied that the cease-fire had ended. On the **25th** the Provisionals said there had been Army harassment of civilians and the IRA would take action against such violations of the truce agreement.

2 October 12 people died in a series of bombings and shootings carried out by the UVF. The next day the organisation was again proscribed, and on the **21st** reports suggested that a new Brigade staff had taken control, claiming that the present policies were totally contrary to the principles on which the UVF was formed. The Protestant Action Force (PAF), which had claimed responsibility for many sectarian murders, was widely believed to be connected to the UVF. An article in *Fortnight* said: 'The last vestiges of 'politicisation' seem to have evaporated (and the UVF re-established) as the most feared, most anti-Catholic and least predictable loyalist organisation.'

29 October Provisional IRA attacks on members of the Official Republicans, leaving one dead and 17 injured, heralded the beginning of yet another Republican feud. By the time a cease-fire was announced on **13 November**, 11 people had been killed. The UDA/UVF feud opened up again on **15 November** after a UDA member was shot dead.

4 November At Westminster Merlyn Rees announced that 'special category status' was to cease. The ending of 'special category status' was to be part of a policy of 'criminalisation' , which had as its intention the presentation of the IRA as an unrepresentative group of criminals. A further extension of this policy was to be a process unofficially known as 'Ulsterisation', by which the British Army was gradually withdrawn from the primary role in the fight against the IRA and replaced by the RUC.

12 November Merlyn Rees announced that the incident centres, set up to monitor the cease-fire, were to be closed. The cease-fire itself was becoming increasingly meaningless, and the IRA were gradually returning to the offensive.

30 November Eleven prominent members of the IRSP resigned, denouncing the present programme as 'objectively indistinguishable from either wing of the Republican Movement and possibly combining the worst elements of both... the IRSP has consistently attempted to downgrade the struggle for class politics and reverted to the sterile nationalism of traditional Republicanism'.

5 December Detention without trial was ended.

19 December 4 people were murdered in Loyalist bombings in South Armagh and across the border in Dundalk, and on **31 December** 3 people were killed when a Protestant public house in County Down was bombed by a group calling itself the Armagh People's Republican Army.

Death toll for the year: 220 civilians, 15 Army, and 14 RUC & UDR.

1976

4 January 5 Catholics were killed by Loyalist gunmen in South Armagh.

5 January 12 gunmen, claiming to be from the Republican Action Force, stopped a busload of workmen near Kingsmills, South Armagh, made the only Catholic step aside and then shot 10 Protestants dead. The following day it was announced that the British government was sending 600 men of the 'Spearhead' battalion into South Armagh. On the **7th** it was announced that units of the Special Air Service (SAS) were being sent to South Armagh for patrolling and surveillance. 48 people were to die violently this month.

9 January Several thousand workers marched through Lurgan in protest at the sectarian murders that had taken place in the South Armagh area.

7 February William Craig called for a broadly based government in Northern Ireland that could unite the greatest number of people.

12 February At the Convention the SDLP withdrew after claiming that the UUUC were not prepared to discuss power-sharing. In England IRA hunger striker, Frank Stagg, died in Wakefield prison; he had gone on hunger strike when the Home Office refused to transfer him to a prison in Northern Ireland. His death was followed by widespread rioting in Belfast.

1 March With the phasing out of special category status, any prisoner convicted of offences committed after today was to be treated as an ordinary criminal. To implement this, Long Kesh prison was divided into what were essentially two separate prisons: the Maze(Compound), with Nissen huts, popularly known as the 'Cages', which would continue to hold the dwindling number of special category prisoners convicted before the cut-off date, and the Maze(Cellular) a new complex of buildings that would hold the new wave of inmates, designed in the shape of an 'H' - the H-Blocks.

4 March After the failure of the Northern Ireland Convention, Westminster formally dissolved it.

10 March Sammy Smyth, a UDA leader, was shot dead in North Belfast.

8 April The murder of a prison warder marked the start of an IRA campaign of assassination of warders in protest at the ending of political status.

6 May In the Republic, the Criminal Law (Jurisdiction) Bill, designed to allow persons accused of terrorist offences in Britain to be tried in Ireland, and vice versa, became law.

17 May After the Provisionals had threatened that it would be a long hot summer for the RUC, the UDA said that 'the long hot summer can work both ways'.

5 June 8 people died in a series of 'tit-for-tat' murders, as the killings continued without let-up.

6 June Paddy Devlin, SDLP, argued that one of the advantages of an independent Northern Ireland was that it would get rid of the British presence and so remove any excuse for the continuing paramilitary violence.

21 July Christopher Ewart-Biggs, British Ambassador to Ireland, and Judith Cooke, a civil servant, were killed when a bomb exploded under their car.

26 July Republican and Loyalist prisoners made a joint protest against the recently-introduced 'strip-searches'.

10 August When an IRA member was shot dead by soldiers pursuing his car in Finaghy Road North, Belfast, the vehicle went out of control and crushed a mother and her children against railings, three of the children being killed.

12 August Over a 1,000 women gathered at the spot where the children died. 6,000 people signed a peace petition organised by Andersonstown women.

14 August 10,000 people took part in a peace rally in Finaghy Road North attended by several busloads of women from the Shankill Road. After the rally, those attending were harassed by Provisional sympathisers.

21 August 20,000 people gathered for a peace rally in Ormeau Park, Belfast.

26 August The European Commission on Human Rights found the British Government guilty of using torture after the introduction of Internment in August 1971.

28 August Over 20,000 people marched up the Shankill Road as part of the developing campaign of the Women's Peace Movement (which later became the Peace People).

4 September 25,000 people from all over the province attended a Peace rally in Derry. 150 Sinn Fein supporters staged a simultaneous counter-protest.

11/12 September Peace rallies were held in Antrim, Coleraine, Strabane, Craigavon, Dungannon, Newtownards and Ballynahinch in Northern Ireland, and Drogheda, Waterford, Dundalk, Longford, Kilkenny, Ennis, Nenagh and Gorey in the Irish Republic.

14 September Women supporters of the Peace Movement who tried to prevent hijacking on the Shankill Road, Belfast, were pelted with eggs by local youths (and on **5 October** two daughters of Peace Women were beaten up in a Shankill Road bar). The DUP said the Peace Movement was 'counter-productive'.

16 September Ciaran Nugent, an IRA member who had been arrested in May, and was the first to be convicted for a terrorist offence committed after the cut-off date for special category status, when asked for his clothes' size at the Maze prison, so that he could be issued with a uniform, replied: 'You must be joking me.' Refusing to wear prison clothes, he returned to his cell wrapped only in a blanket, and the 'blanket' protest had begun. By **May 1977** there were 80 prisoners 'on the blanket'. (18)

10 October Three Peace leaders were attacked in Turf Lodge, Belfast, and had their cars wrecked, by people protesting at the killing of a 13-year-old boy by an Army plastic bullet.

23 October Provisional Sinn Fein supporters attacked a Peace People's march on the Falls Road, Belfast, and 16 people had to be taken to hospital.

28 October Maire Drumm, former Vice-President of Provisional Sinn Fein, was shot dead by Loyalist gunmen while in the Mater Hospital.

7 November 1,662 white crosses were planted in the grounds of Belfast City Hall in memory of those who had been killed in the present 'troubles'.

November The Provisional IRA Army Council gave its approval to the establishment of a supplementary organisation in the North, the Northern Command, which held its first meeting this month. Disillusionment within the IRA about the cease-fire - it was breached constantly by the Northern units - accompanied by a decline in the authority of the Southern-based leadership of O'Bradaigh and O'Connaill, was partly behind this new development. (2)

3 December In London the House of Commons was told that the housing situation in Belfast was 'certainly the worst in the UK and probably the worst in Europe'.

12 December The Ulster Loyalist Co-Ordinating Committee said that certain Loyalist politicians, who weren't named, were guilty in the past of gun-running, selecting bomb targets and promising money to buy arms.

21 December The unemployment figure for Northern Ireland (at 10.4%) was the worst December total for 36 years.

Death toll for the year: 243 civilians, 14 Army, and 38 RUC & UDR. It was the worst death toll since 1972.

1977

6 January The Peace People, in a document entitled *Strategy for Peace*, suggested that there should be a non-political party 'Assembly' made up of community groups, which would in turn elect an 'Executive'.

20 January The Provisional IRA said that even if they had to pull Belfast down brick by brick, they would eventually remove 'the British presence'.

2 February The Provisional IRA shot dead the head of the Du Pont Corporation in Derry, and two more businessmen in the following weeks. In a later statement the IRA said: 'In all cases, those executed by the IRA played a prominent role in the effort to stabilize the British-oriented Six County economy.'

March The killings from both Republicans and Loyalists continued without let-up, one UDR victim being shot dead in front of his two children, another man from Ardoyne being shot four times in the back while trying to shield the body of his 4-year-old son, and following a previous statement from the Provisionals that the immediate families of policemen were now 'legitimate targets', a 63-year-old mother of a RUC Reservist was shot dead.

3 April At a conference to elect a steering committee for the Peace People, Ciaran McKeown said: 'We should be prepared for worsening violence, because as community support decreases for the men of violence they will be left with only their naked militarism to make themselves felt. Their acts of violence will probably become more desperate than even those we have seen so far, and we must be prepared for this. We have turned the corner, and the war is beginning to disintegrate. There is less idealism or strategy now, but there are a great many people with arms and the trouble will probably stagger on for a couple of years.'

4 April Peace People leader Betty Williams revealed that dozens of prisoners from all shades of the paramilitary spectrum had been requesting secret visits from members of the Peace movement. These visits had been going on for four months.

8 April The Provisionals announced that civilian searchers at security checkpoints would be considered as 'part of the British occupation forces'.

10 April A 10-year-old boy was killed and a teenager lost a leg when a bomb went off at a Republican Clubs gathering. The dead boy's uncle was shot dead by 3 gunmen when he went to inform relatives. The Republican Clubs blamed the attacks on the Provisionals, and Provisional supporters later attacked Republican Club marchers at Milltown Cemetery. In his Easter sermon the Roman Catholic Bishop of Derry, Dr. Edward Daly, in a reference to proposals for integrated education, said it was a libel to allege that Catholic schools were a prime cause of keeping people apart in Northern Ireland. He said that the real source of division in northern society was the fact that centuries of injustice were inflicted on one section of the people because they refused to give up their religious beliefs. He also said that he would resist any attempt to change the character of Catholic schools.

29 April Plans by Rev. Ian Paisley and the United Ulster Action Council for a general strike in protest at the lack of a proper security 'offensive' against the IRA, received a set-back when shipyard workers voted not to support the stoppage. Official Unionist, Vanguard and Orange Order leaders had already expressed their opposition to it.

30 April Rev. Ian Paisley told supporters in Ballymena that if the Ulster people refused to back the strike he would quit politics: 'I did not choose political life. I went into it because of the call of the people and have sought honestly to fulfil my pledge... The strike will not be called off. It will not be for 24 hours - it will be on until we get victory... The security forces must go into IRA territory - their very breeding places - and root them out, lock, stock and barrel.' As people stocked up with food bakeries were working flat out to meet the demand. O'Hara's were delivering bread to their shops every two hours. Some shops were rationing sales to two loaves per customer.

3 May The first day of the strike saw many factories remaining open, and police responded to numerous complaints alleging intimidation. On the **4th** the police clashed with the UDA in East Belfast, and Andy Tyrie, Chairman of the UDA, had a confrontation with RUC officers outside UDA headquarters.

6 May The strikers failed to get the support of the Ballylumford power station workers for the stoppage.

13 May The strike was finally called off. Although it was widely considered to be a failure, Rev. Paisley said he felt it had been a success, and he would be continuing in politics.

17 May The Provisional IRA and the UDA denied being party to talks between Belfast barrister Desmond Boal and former Foreign Minister of the Irish Republic Sean McBride, after a TV programme claimed the two men had been asked to mediate in peace talks between the paramilitary orgnisations. Peter Robinson of the DUP said: 'The people of Ulster have only one message for the IRA. We seek your elimination. No-one who talks to the IRA represents the Loyalists of Ulster.' It was later revealed that some Loyalist individuals had requested that the two men explore if there was any common ground for a settlement.

12 June At Provisional Sinn Fein's annual Wolfe Tone commemoration ceremony at Bodenstown, those assembled were told that, despite earlier impressions, the British were not withdrawing after all, and the Republican struggle would require 'the mobilisation of the working class in the Twenty-six Counties'. Jimmy Drumm also told the crowd: 'We say that the first and paramount right of any Irish citizen - nay the God-given right - is the right to decide their own destiny without outside interference. We will not plead for this; we will take what is ours by right.'

15 July From the Maze prison, former UVF leader Gusty Spence said that Loyalist politicians were a 'sick joke', and suggested a 'summit conference' of paramilitaries. He also said that Ulster was the 'most socially and legalistically oppressive country in the western hemisphere'. On the **16th** the UVF said that Spence's views were his own and not those of the UVF.

18 July A government report said that the infant mortality rate in Northern Ireland was the highest in the UK, and among the highest in the Common Market.

23 July John McKeague, of the Ulster Independence Association, said: 'Everybody should get round a table and accept that the British are going. The days of the Orange Order and the Orange card are over.'

26 July Unemployment figures of 13% were the highest in the province since 1938. In Britain the figure was 6.8%.

27 July Feuding broke out between the Official and Provisional IRA leaving 4 dead and 19 injured. The next day a cease-fire was arranged, but a futher 6 were injured.

10 August The Queen began a 2-day visit to the province, when the Royal Yacht Britannia anchored in Belfast Lough. The SDLP declined to meet her.

27 September Paddy Devlin, expelled recently from the SDLP for complaining that the party was reducing the socialist content of its policy, described it s expression of concern for equal distribution of wealth as 'claptrap'.

5 October The leader of the IRSP was shot dead in his car in Dublin.

10 October Mairead Corrigan and Betty Williams of the Peace People were awarded the Nobel Peace Prize for 1976.

October Residents in the Clonard area of West Belfast prevented IRA members dropping concrete blocks on the limbs of a local teenager. The Provisionals issued a statement saying: 'Local people in Dunmore Street interfered when a unit of volunteers was about to apprehend one of the worst criminals in the Clonard area. As a result of this interference, the lives and liberty of the volunteers were put in jeopardy. We wish to make it absolutely and emphatically clear to the people of Dunmore Street and the whole of Clonard area that this interference will not be tolerated in the future and that anyone, young or old, male or female, who obstructs the volunteer in this work will be shot.'

10 December Peace People leaders Mairead Corrigan and Betty Williams received their Nobel Peace Prize at a ceremony at Oslo University. On their return from Norway they led a rally through Belfast on the **17th**, but Belfast City Council decided not to honour them with a civic reception.

Death toll for the year: 67 civilians, 15 Army and 28 RUC & UDR.

1978

15 January The Roman Catholic Primate of Ireland, Tomas O Fiaich, in a newspaper interview, said: 'I think the British should withdraw from Ireland... I think it's the only way which will get things moving.'

18 January The European Court of Human Rights in Strasbourg ruled that the interrogation methods used on internees in 1971 did not constitute torture, but had been 'inhuman and degrading'.

22 January 1,000 people attended an 'anti-repression' conference held in

Coalisland, organised by Bernadette McAliskey and members of the Tyrone Relatives Action Committee (these Action Committees had been formed in 1976 to publicise the H-Block issue), and it was decided to organise marches and petitions on behalf of the prisoners. While representatives of Provisional Sinn Fein attended, they were sceptical about the broad-based 'united front' proposed by the conference. On **4 February** *Republican News* said: 'Any public campaign against torture and for political status needs to be pointed firmly in the direction of 'Brits Out', and needs to recognise the necessary methods for this aim. For status and torture in reality cannot be isolated from the Brit presence: a presence which cannot be removed without armed struggle.' In a statement to the *Derry Journal* (**18 May**), Sinn Fein called the H-Block campaign 'an issue deliberately created by the British regime to direct people, time and energy, from the main goal of national liberation'. A letter to *Republican News* (**23 April**) asked why Sinn Fein should bother to woo 'the lunatic fringe, the cast-offs and rejects of the political spectrum?'

January The New Ulster Political Research Group (NUPRG), under the chairmanship of Glen Barr, was formed by leading members of the UDA.

11 February In Dublin Garrett Fitzgerald, the Fine Gael leader, said that Ulster Protestants would be 'bloody fools' to join with the Irish Republic under its present constitution.

17 February 12 people were burned to death and over 30 injured when the La Mon Restaurant outside Belfast was bombed by the IRA. The explosion created a fireball which swept through the building in seconds.

March In the Maze prison, in a dispute between prisoners and staff, prisoners refused to leave their cells to go to the washrooms - this was the beginning of the 'no wash protest'. Following on from this, in a dispute over the emptying of their chamber pots, prisoners resorted to smearing excrement on the walls, and the 'dirty protest' had begun, which by the summer involved over 250 Republican prisoners.

27 April David Payne, former UDA commander for North Belfast, was wounded in his home by Loyalist gunmen. He had recently spoken to a meeting of the Peace People.

10 May A Republican prisoner, Brian Maguire, was found hanged in his cell at

Castlereagh interrogation centre. The RUC said that he had committed suicide. Rioting followed the news of his death for three nights. On the **12th** the Chief Constable announced an inquiry into the death.

13 June Amnesty International, in a report on RUC treatment of suspects, found that there was consistent evidence of malpractice by the plain clothes branch of the RUC.

30 July Archbishop Tomas O Fiaich visited the H-Blocks and was appalled at the conditions of those on the 'dirty protest'. In a statement afterwards he said: 'One would hardly allow an animal to remain in such conditions, let alone a human being. The stench and filth in some of the cells, with the remains of rotten food and human excreta scattered around the walls, was almost unbearable. In two of them I was unable to speak for fear of vomiting. Several prisoners complained to me of beatings, of verbal abuse, of additional punishments (in cold cells without even a mattress) for making complaints, and of degrading searches carried out on the most intimate parts of their naked bodies. Of course I have no way of verifying these allegations, but they were numerous.' He found the men's morale high: 'It was an indication of the triumph of the human spirit over adverse material conditions to notice Irish words, phrases and songs being shouted from cell to cell and then written on each cell wall with the remnants of toothpaste tubes.' The reply from the NIO said: 'These criminals are totally responsible for the situation in which they find themselves. It is they who have been smearing excreta on the walls and pouring urine through cell doors. It is they who by their actions are denying themselves the excellent modern facilities of the prison. They are not political prisoners: more than 80 have been convicted of murder or attempted murder, and more than 80 of explosive offences. They are members of organisations responsible for the deaths of hundreds of innocent people, the maiming of thousands more and the torture, by knee-capping, of more than 600 of their own people.'

2 August It was announced that the De Lorean Motor Company was to manufacture luxury sports cars at a factory at Twinbrook, Lisburn. Of the £65m involved the government was to supply £56m. While the creation of between 800 and 1,500 new jobs was generally welcomed, there were doubts raised as to the viability of the project.

2 September After H-Block demonstrations had attracted crowds of up to 15,000, coverage in *Republican News* seemed to indicate that Provisional

Sinn Fein had finally overcome its original hesitancy about the campaign: 'Every drop of publicity has been hard won. It has been wrung out of the mass media by protest after protest by 'blanket-clad' women occupying buildings, blocking roads, and carrying out token hunger strikes, and by foot-slogging the streets in cities, towns and villages from one end of Ireland to the other, handing out leaflets detailing the horrific conditions Republican prisoners are held in.'

14 November Bombs throughout the province injured 37 people.

26 November Albert Myles, deputy governor of the Maze prison, was shot dead at his North Belfast home by the IRA.

18 December 24 hours after the Provisionals launched bombing attacks on 5 British cities, car bombs exploded in London. In Belfast, 5 RUC men were charged with the murder of a Catholic shopkeeper and the kidnapping of a priest. The priest had been abducted after the IRA kidnapped a policeman.

December The SDLP launched a 'New Ireland' campaign in the hope of convincing the British government that a permanent solution to the problems of Northern Ireland could only be achieved in an Irish context.

Death toll for the year: 50 civilians, 14 Army and 17 RUC & UDR.

1979

1 January The IRA planted bombs throughout the province.

20 February A Loyalist murder gang responsible for 19 killings, and known as the 'Shankill Butchers', were convicted and sentenced.

11 March Dr. Robert Irwin, Forensic Medical Officer and Secretary to the NI Police Surgeons' Association, claimed that up to 150 people he had seen during the course of his work at Castlereagh interrogation centre bore evidence of having been physically ill-treated by RUC detectives. He was supported by Jack Hassard who had recently resigned from the NI Police Authority after making similar allegations. Dr. Denis Elliott, Chief Medical

Officer at the Armagh interrogation centre resigned too, claiming that he could no longer work under the conditions prevailing there. On the16th the government finally published the long-delayed Bennett Report into 'Police Interrogation Procedures in Northern Ireland'. It found that 'there was prime facie evidence that ill-treatment had taken place'. The report was accepted by Roy Mason, Secretary of State, who promised immediate action on some of the findings, including the installation of closed circuit TV's to monitor interrogations.

3 March The Provisional IRA admitted killing two 16-year-old boys and injuring three others (one boy losing an arm), all of whom were on their way to a dance in Keady, County Armagh. The IRA statement said that one of their units had been lying in wait for the security forces, and continued: 'Tragically the youths, and their positions on the road, were mistaken for the movement of soldiers, and the bomb was set off.' The IRA offered its 'deepest sympathy' to the families.

22 March The British Ambassador to Holland, Sir Richard Sykes, was shot dead in the Hague. The IRA later claimed responsibility.

23 March 24 bombs went off throughout the province.

29 March The NUPRG, the study group set up by the UDA, published *Beyond the Religious Divide*. In it they said: 'Without the evolution of proper politics the people of Northern Ireland will continually be manipulated by sectarian politicians who make no contribution to the social and economic well-being of the people of the country, but only continue to fan the flames of religious bigotry for self gain and preservation.' They suggested that the only way 'proper politics' could emerge would be to have both Britain and Southern Ireland 'withdraw all their claims of sovereignty over Northern Ireland', and for the two communities to work together for Negiotated Independence, which would encourage the development of their common identity. To the people of Northern Ireland they commended the words of Bacon: 'He who cannot compromise is a fool; he who will not compromise is a bigot; he who dare not compromise is a slave.'

31 March In London, Airey Neave, Conservative spokesman on Northern Ireland, was killed when his car was blown up as he was leaving the House of Commons. The INLA claimed responsibility.

17 April 4 RUC members were killed at Bessbrook, County Armagh, when a 1,000 lb bomb in a van exploded as they drove past in their Land Rover.

7 June In the election to the European Parliament the following three politicians were elected: Rev. Ian Paisley, who received 170,668 first preference votes; John Hume, who received 140,622 first preference votes; and John Taylor, who received 68,185 first preference votes.

12 July Cardinal Tomas O Fiaich received confirmation that his invitation to Pope John Paul II to visit Ireland had been accepted. It was hoped the Pope would be able to include a visit to Northern Ireland.

23 July The Church of Ireland Bishop of Conor, Dr. Arthur Butler, deplored the attitude taken by Rev. Paisley (who had called for the Pope to be banned from visiting Northern Ireland). Dr. Butler said that his own first reaction was of real pleasure for the sake of the Roman Catholic community in Ireland.

24 July The Presbyterian Moderator, Dr. William Craig, said he was unwilling to meet the Pope during his visit to Ireland, 'not from any personal feelings or animosities, but from theological convictions'.

25 July Rev. Paisley, replying to criticism of his stance on the Pope's visit, said: 'I have the right to speak for the Protestant people of Ulster, for I have a mandate from them while these clergy have only ecclesiastical officialdom.'

26 July Father Des Wilson, in response to Rev. Paisley, said: 'If he can tell us who we can or cannot see then we will never have peace in my lifetime. From now on we must accept every challenge which this man puts down. He has got to be told once and for all that his bullying days are over.' In the Republic, the Fine Gael spokesman on Northern Ireland said that seldom, if ever, had anyone been such a good public relations officer for the Provisionals as Rev. Ian Paisley. He added that at a time when the IRA propaganda machine was flagging and their credibility at home and abroad was becoming stale, overspent and overplayed, up out of Pandora's box jumped 'the Bible-thumping parson'.

31 July The Grand Orange Lodge of Ireland criticised the proposed visit to Northern Ireland by the Pope, saying that it 'regrets that the occasion should promote the unacceptable face of Romanism'. 'As a body which believes and practices civil and religious liberty, we will use the opportunity for the Protestants of Northern Ireland to spell out clearly their concern at the glaring silence of successive Pontiffs, and the obvious acquiescence of the Roman sacramental system, in the rape of Ulster with the murder of our citizens and the destruction of our property.' Despite such Protestant hostility to a papal visit to the province, the UDA and Loyalist leaders like John McKeague had assured Cardinal O Fiaich that the Pope could visit wherever he liked, and a visit to Armagh was finally included in the itinerary.

3 August The US State Department said it was banning the sale of guns to the RUC until it had reviewed its policy regarding the force. The decision followed pressure from the Irish-American lobby in Congress.

27 August In the Republic, in the waters off Mullaghmore in County Sligo an IRA bomb exploded on a boat containing Earl Mountbatton and members of his family. Mountbatton, his grandson, Lady Brabourne, and a 15-year-old Enniskillen boy, were all killed. In Northern Ireland, near Narrow Water Castle outside Warrenpoint, 6 British soldiers were killed by a remote control IRA bomb. As the survivors of the attack took up positions behind a nearby wall, a second bomb hidden there was exploded and the death toll finally rose to 18. Cardinal Tomas O Fiaich had just arrived in Rome to discuss the details of the Pope's visit when he heard the news. He later said: 'At one point it came through that there were six dead and there were ten dead and then there were twelve dead. I could just feel the ground crumbling under my feet.' (2) When O Fiaich contacted the Irish bishops the feeling was that the Pope's visit to Armagh had to be cancelled.

2 September The UFF announced that a murder campaign would begin against known Republicans.

29 September In the Irish Republic, Pope John Paul II addressed a crowd estimated at around 250,000 at Drogheda. In his speech he said: 'Now I wish to speak to all men and women engaged in violence. I appeal to you in language of passionate pleading. On my knees I beg you to turn away from the paths of violence and return to the paths of peace. You may claim to seek justice. I too believe in justice and seek justice. But violence always delays the day of justice. Violence destroys the work of justice.'

2 October The Provisionals in a statement rejected the Pope's plea for an end to violence, saying that the British presence could only be removed by force.

74

21 October A new campaign was launched to bring about the restoration of special category status by the National H-Block/Armagh Committee, which included members of Sinn Fein, the IRSP, and sympathisers such as Bernadette McAliskey (formerly Devlin). While the prisoners themselves were demanding political status, the H-Block committee decided to call instead for 5 demands to be met: the right of the prisoners to wear their own clothes, to refuse prison work, to receive one parcel and one visit per week, to associate freely with one another and to have the remission lost for being on the blanket protest returned.

20 November The British government published a consultative document for a proposed Northern Ireland 'constitutional conference'. A meeting of SDLP constituency representatives rejected it because it ruled out any 'Irish dimension' and 'reduced power-sharing to a mere option'. Gerry Fitt had welcomed it earlier in the day, but now agreed to withdraw his favourable comments.

21 November SDLP constituency representatives met again with the party executive, and upheld their criticism of Gerry Fitt for having made a statement without first consulting the party. On the **22nd** Gerry Fitt resigned. He said he felt the party's attitude was 'disastrous and completely misguided'. On the **28th** John Hume was elected leader, and Seamus Mallon deputy leader.

23 November OUP leader James Molyneaux received overwhelming support from his executive for refusing to attend the proposed conference. With reference to a letter Humphrey Atkins had written to the SDLP urging them to attend, Molyneaux said it showed that the conference was 'booby-trapped' with the 'Irish dimension'.

26 November The Provisionals hit the province with a bomb blitz, 24 of the bombs going off in Belfast.

29 November The Secretary of State postponed the conference and appealed to both the SDLP and the Official Unionists to participate.

3 December The second-in-command to the Governor of Crumlin Road prison was shot dead outside his home. He was the 16th member of the prison service to be killed in the IRA's campaign of retaliation for the denial of political status.

5 December Jack Lynch resigned as Taoiseach and Fine Fail leader. On the **7th** Charles Haughey became leader. On the **9th** Andy Tyrie, UDA leader, said he would be prepared to meet Haughey. On **16 April 1980** members of the NUPRG met with Haughey in Dublin.

Death toll for the year: 51 civilians, 38 Army and 24 RUC & UDR.

1980

7 January The constitutional conference finally convened with the DUP, SDLP and Alliance Party attending. The SDLP had been told that they could engage in 'parallel talks' with the Secretary of State to discuss matters not covered by the conference. The conference adjourned on **24 March**, and held its final session on **18 April**.

17 January The government announced that 2 blocks of Divis Flats, at the bottom of the Falls Road in Belfast, built in the sixties, were to be pulled down. A local community group, the Divis Demolition Group, said that their struggle would go on to have the whole complex demolished.

19 January At the Provisional Sinn Fein ard fheis a letter from the men in the H-Blocks was read out which said that although their commitment to the blanket campaign was still high they couldn't hold out for ever.

21 January Anne Maguire, the mother of the 3 children whose deaths had sparked off the Women's Peace Movement, took her own life. Her suicide, described as 'one of the most poignant deaths' of all the province's fatalities, followed repeated bouts of depression. The only child to have survived the earlier tragedy, her 9-year-old-son, discovered something was wrong when he couldn't get into the house on his return from school, and went to fetch neighbours. Her close friend Betty Williams, one of the founders of the Peace Movement, weeping bitterly, said: 'It was horrible. My wee Anne is dead. We tried so hard to help her. How a woman can lose one child, let alone three, and not suffer terribly.' The Maguires had tried to make a new start in New Zealand, but had returned because of homesickness, accompanied by a new daughter named after their dead one.

1 February The Belfast Welfare Rights Poverty survey revealed that Northern Ireland was the poorest region in the UK. In **June** a further study, *Ends That Won't Meet*, by the Child Poverty Action Group, said: 'The striking volume of income deprivation is a product of high unemployment, low wages, higher prices and slightly larger households. No other region in the United Kingdom is trying to cope with the combined effects of such a range of problems. Alongside (these) is a severe housing problem - again unique in its nature and proportions. 2,000 jobs have recently been lost, 16,000 jobs (in shipbuilding and man-made fibres) are in jeopardy, and trade union estimates put the total number of jobs at risk as in excess of 30,000.'

11 February Amid reports of a split among members of the Executive of the Peace People, Betty Williams resigned. On **5 March** the former chairman Peter McLachlan also resigned.

3 March Cardinal Thomas O Fiaich and Dr. Edward Daly, Bishop of Derry, visited the Maze prison. On **1 April** they both met the Secretary of State to discuss the prison issue.

26 March Humphrey Atkins offered minor concessions to the H-Block prisoners. They would be permitted to exercise in sports clothing, and could receive one extra visit per month. This was rejected by the prisoners.

31 March Following the shooting dead of a teenage 'joyrider' in a stolen car, there was widespread concern about this growing activity by young people.

3 April 3 staff members at the Kincora Boys' Home in East Belfast were charged with acts of gross indecency with some of the inmates. On **18 February 1982** James Prior announced a public inquiry into the Kincora affair. In **March 1982** there were allegations that British Intelligence had been aware of the homosexual and political activities of one of the former Kincora staff members in 1973. On **28 October 1983** Sir George Terry in a report said he found no evidence that the RUC, military intelligence or British civil servants were involved in the scandal or had tried to cover it up. Commentators in the media continued to express doubts.

21 May Taoiseach Charles Haughey and British Prime Minister Margaret Thatcher held talks in London, and agreed to closer political co-operation.

19 June The European Commission on Human Rights rejected the case of the protesting prisoners at the Maze. It found that the debasement of the 'dirty protest' was 'self-inflicted', and 'designed to create maximum sympathy and to enlist public support for their political aims'. 'The Commission must observe that the applicants are seeking to achieve a status of political prisoner which they are not entitled to under national law or under the (European) Convention.'

26 June Dr. Miriam Daly, a member of the National H-Blocks Committee, was shot dead by UFF gunmen.

2 July The British government published its 'Discussion Document' on the future government of Northern Ireland. Political commentators didn't see much hope for an agreement.

10 October With the H-Block campaign outside the prison stagnating, and attendances at protest marches falling, the prisoners announced they were commencing a hunger strike on the **27th**.

15 October Two prominent members of the IRSP, one of them the son of the prominent Loyalist, Major Ronald Bunting, were assassinated by UFF gunmen.

23 October The NIO announced that prisoners in Northern Ireland would be allowed to wear 'civilian-style' clothes provided by the authorities. The prisoners rejected this as 'meaningless'.

27 October Seven Republican prisoners refused meals on the first day of their 'fast to the death'. There were now 342 prisoners involved in the 'dirty' protest. The next day Mrs Thatcher confirmed that political status would not be granted to the hunger strikers.

2 November Provisional Sinn Fein organised demonstrations throughout Ireland about the H-Blocks. Sinn Fein President, Ruairi O'Bradaigh, referred to the prison issue as 'a showdown with imperialism'.

10 November In a speech to the House of Commons, Gerry Fitt, Independent Socialist, warned the government not to grant concessions to the hunger strikers, and criticised Cardinal O Fiaich and Bishop Daly for their statements, which he claimed only encouraged the Provisionals to proceed with the fast.

13 November Paddy O'Hanlon, SDLP, said that in return for concessions the IRA should call a cease-fire, adding that it was 'hypocritical to talk in agonised terms about the hunger strikers and at the same time to kill people on the outside'.

4 December The Secretary of State, Humphrey Atkins, made a statement to the House of Commons declaring that there would be no concessions to the hunger strikers. Atkins met John Hume, SDLP, for talks about the H-Block issue.

8 December Mrs Thatcher, Humphrey Atkins, Lord Carrington (the British Foreign Minister), and Geoffry Howe (Chancellor of the Exchequer) met with Charles Haughey, Brian Lenihan (Irish Minister for Foreign Affairs) and Michael O'Kennedy (Minister for Finance) in Dublin. This very top-level meeting agreed that 'Anglo-Irish Studies' would examine possible new institutional structures, citizenship rights, security matters, economic co-operation, and measures to encourage mutual understanding.

15 December 23 more prisoners joined the hunger strike (3 women from Armagh prison had joined on the **1st**). 7 more joined the following day.

17 December The NIO said that hunger striker Sean McKenna was 'deteriorating rapidly'.

18 December The original 7 hunger strikers, apparently in the belief that following discussions with the NIO there was now the possibility of a solution, ended their fast.

19 December Gerry Adams, at a celebration march, said that although the hunger strike had been 'a victory', it would be well to remain 'vigilant, alert, and patient'.

Death toll for the year: 50 civilians, 8 Army and 18 RUC & UDR.

1981

1 January 2 men died of stab wounds in Bawnmore estate, Belfast, during a street battle involving separate families.

10 January An RUC Reservist was shot in the head in central Belfast (he died on the **14th**).

16 January A part-time UDR major was shot dead in Warrenpoint customs post where he worked. Bernadette McAliskey and her husband were shot and seriously wounded in their County Tyrone home by UDA gunmen. The gunmen were caught by an undercover Army patrol that had been keeping watch on the house.

20 January One British soldier was killed and another seriously injured as they were closing the security gates in Derry. In South Armagh the body of an Ardoyne man was found; the IRA claimed they had shot him as an informer.

21 January Sir Norman Stronge, former Speaker of the Stormont Parliament, was shot dead by the IRA along with his son at their home, Tynan Abbey; the building was also destroyed by a bomb. In Belfast, a Protestant was shot at his workplace on the Glen Road; his Catholic workmates walked out in protest at the shooting.

24 January A British soldier was shot dead by the IRA in Belfast city centre.

26 January 12 people were injured in a spate of bombings.

27 January 96 Republican prisoners, who claimed that the prison authorities were refusing to issue them with their own clothes, broke furniture and smashed windows in their cells.

30 January A part-time UDR member was seriously injured in a gun attack in County Tyrone.

31 January Andy Tyrie, Supreme Commander of the UDA, said that the terrorists should be 'terrorised', and that the UDA might decide to pursue them over the border. Following this statement there were renewed demands for the UDA to be proscribed.

2 February Senior British and Irish government officials began their first 'joint studies' session.

5 February The Republican Press Office in Belfast announced that there would be a new hunger strike beginning on **1 March**.

6 February An RUC Reservist was shot dead and a colleague seriously injured in an ambush in South Belfast. Five journalists were taken to a remote hillside in County Antrim where Rev. Ian Paisley displayed 500 men with firearms certificates. He said that the 'men of Ulster' were organising themselves to resist to the death 'the process of ongoing all-Ireland integration intended to flow from the Dublin summit'. This display was condemned by government officials and other Unionist leaders.

8 February A part-time UDR member was murdered in his East Belfast shop by the INLA.

9 February Rev. Paisley launched a Carson-style 'Covenant' in Belfast City Hall.

10 February In Derry, a part-time UDR member was shot dead at his workplace.

13 February The first 'Carson Trail' meeting was held in Omagh Orange Hall. On **17 February** Sir Edward Carson's son said: 'I dislike intensely the way my father's name is being used.'

18 February The trustees of Carson Orange Hall in Portadown refused to let it be used by the DUP for a meeting.

22 February In Andersonstown the Provisional IRA shot dead a man they claimed was an informer; he was the fourth member of his family to die in the troubles.

23 February A man was shot dead in West Belfast ten days after receiving a suspended sentence for the manslaughter of his wife. Rev. Ian Paisley produced a bandolier at a 'Carson Trail' rally in Portadown.

25 February The Secretary of State repeated assurances that there would be no 'sell-out' of the Union in the Anglo-Irish talks.

1 March Five years to the day that 'special category status' had ended, Bobby Sands, serving 14 years for firearms and other offences, began a hunger strike. The next day the 'dirty protest' was called off to focus attention on the hunger strike.

5 March Frank Maguire, Independent MP for Fermanagh/South Tyrone, died of a heart attack. Rev. Paisley told a 'Carson Trail' rally in Enniskillen that the 500 men he displayed in February were only a token of the 150,000 he had all over the province. Gerry Fitt was to say: 'In Northern Ireland people of all political persuasions are convinced that the TV documentaries now being shown have had a dramatic effect on Mr. Paisley. He is now convinced he is a second Carson. He walks like Carson and he talks like Carson.'

11 March The Ministry of Defence began building a permanent brick wall - a 'Peace Line' - that would divide the Falls and Shankill Roads in Belfast.

15 March Francis Hughes, convicted for murder, joined the hunger strike.

19 March A man was shot dead while driving the car of a friend who was in the UDR. The Provisionals said they 'deeply regretted' the death.

20 March In Belfast the driver of a stolen car was shot dead when the vehicle was fired upon by the UDR.

22 March Raymond McCreesh and Patsy O'Hara (INLA) joined the hunger strike. Brian Lenihan, Irish Minister for Foreign Affairs, said the Anglo-Irish talks could lead to unity in 10 years. Humphrey Atkins responded that this was 'misleading'. The DUP said that Lenihan's remarks vindicated their current campaign.

24 March A British businessman speaking to a conference in Trinty College, Dublin, was shot in the legs by hunger strike supporters.

25 March Councillor Sammy Millar, a UDA member, was seriously injured in his Shankill Road home by an INLA gunman.

26 March Relations of Bobby Sands announced that his name was being put forward as a candidate in the by-election for Fermanagh/South Tyrone. Other anti-Unionist candidates had stood down, on the understanding that the seat was being 'borrowed' by Sands 'to save his life'.

27 March The INLA shot dead a part-time UDR member in Belfast. Later a Catholic from Ardoyne was killed in what was thought to be retaliation. Austin Currie was selected by the SDLP to stand for the by-election (the SDLP withdrew on the **29th**, and were subjected to widespread criticism for doing so).

28 March Rev. Paisley held a 'Carson Trail' rally at Stormont, and on **1 April** he held 3 further night-time hillside rallies.

3 April In County Armagh, an RUC member was killed when a booby-trap bomb went off in his car.

4 April In Derry a woman collecting census forms was shot dead by a gunman.

9 April There was a high turn-out of the electorate (86.8%) in the Fermanagh/South Tryone by-election. Bobby Sands was elected with 30,492 votes. The defeated Unionist candidate, Harry West, said: 'I never thought the decent Catholics of Fermanagh would vote for the gunman.'

11 April Following celebration parades there was rioting in Belfast, Lurgan and Cookstown.

15 April A 15-year-old boy was seriously injured by a plastic bullet in Derry during rioting (he died on the **25th**).

16 April A UDR member was shot dead in a pub in County Tyrone.

19 April Two teenagers were killed by an army Land Rover during rioting in Derry. The Provisionals threatened that if a hunger striker died the violence that would result would make earlier violence look like 'a Buckingham Palace tea-party'.

23 April A former UDR member was shot dead driving his works bus in Armagh. The Pope appealed for peace in Northern Ireland. The Ulster Army Council, a co-ordinating body for Loyalist paramilitaries, was reactivated.

25 April Officials from the European Commission for Human Rights went into the Maze, but as the prisoners had imposed preconditions which the commissioners could not agree to, no meeting took place and they finally left.

27 April An RUC member was killed and 3 others were injured when the INLA booby-trapped a stolen lorry in West Belfast.

28 April A UDR member was shot dead near Castlewellan. A 'defensive mobilisation exercise' by 2,500 UDA men took place on the Shankill Road, Belfast. Both Catholic and Protestant communities were reported to be stockpiling food. UDA commander Andy Tyrie said that 'the UDA should not come into conflict with the Catholic community'. Father John Magee, the Pope's private secretary, visited Bobby Sands.

5 May Bobby Sands died on the 66th day of his hunger strike. In reaction on the streets, a milkman and his 15-year-old son died after their milkfloat was bombarded with bricks by a crowd and crashed.

6 May A policeman was shot dead and an INLA member was killed by his own bomb.

7 May 100,000 people lined the route to Milltown cemetery in Belfast for the funeral of Bobby Sands.

9 May A 14-year-old boy suffered serious head injuries after being hit by a plastic bullet on the Falls Road.

12 May Hunger striker Francis Hughes died on the 59th day of his fast. There was rioting in Belfast and Dublin. An INLA member was shot dead in a gun battle at Divis Flats in Belfast.

13 May A 14-year-old girl from Lenadoon, Belfast, died after being struck by a plastic bullet. Further rioting occurred in Belfast, Derry and Dublin.

14 May A policeman was killed when a rocket hit his vehicle on the Springfield Road, Belfast.

16 May An Ardoyne man was shot dead at his home.

84

17 May The Secretary-General of Amnesty International said they didn't regard the hunger strikers as 'prisoners of conscience', and would therefore not be getting involved.

19 May In County Armagh 5 British soldiers were killed when their armoured car was blown up by an IRA landmine near Bessbrook. An 11-year-old girl from Twinbrook, Belfast, was injured by a plastic bullet (she died on the **22nd**).

21 May Raymond McCreesh and Patsy O'Hara, who had joined the fast together, both died on their 61st day. Cardinal O Fiaich warned the British government that it would face 'the wrath of the whole Nationalist population' if its 'rigid stance' went unchanged. Leading Catholics criticised his statement. In Derry, a man died after being hit by a plastic bullet.

22 May In the local government election results the DUP became the largest Unionist party. IRSP and PD candidates won seats on Belfast City Council.

23 May A man was killed by a police vehicle which was being stoned in the Oldpark Road area of Belfast.

25 May The IRA attacked two UDR vehicles, killing one soldier.

26 May Hunger striker Brendan McLaughlin agreed to accept 'limited' medical aid - he had a perforated ulcer and was bleeding internally. The following day he was taken off the fast 'on medical grounds'.

28 May On a visit to Belfast, the Prime Minister Margaret Thatcher said that 'faced with the failure of their discredited cause, the men of violence have chosen in recent months to play what may well be their last card'.

29 May An off-duty RUC member was shot dead near Newry. In Derry 2 IRA members were killed in a gun battle.

31 May An RUC Reservist was shot dead guarding a patient in the Royal Victoria Hospital in Belfast. A member of the Army bomb disposal team (the 17th to date) was killed by a car-bomb near Newry.

3 June A civilian was killed when the IRA opened fire on the Army in Derry.

5 June Near Lisnaskea, a UDR man was shot dead while delivering coal.

8 June A youth was injured in a 'punishment shooting' in Andersonstown. The RUC estimated that there had been 850 such shootings since 1973.

11 June In a General Election in the Irish Republic, Garrett Fitzgerald became Taoiseach. 2 Maze prisoners were elected as TD's.

17 June An RUC Reservist was fatally wounded near his home in County Tyrone.

21 June A RUC member was shot dead in a Newry public house.

26 June The body of a man shot by the IRA, who alleged he was an informer, was found at Divis Flats.

29 June A communication smuggled out from the prisoners asked: 'What sort of people are we dealing with? It appears they are not interested in simply undermining us, but completely annihilating us. They are insane - at least Maggie is anyway.'

4 July The prisoners issued a statement in which they appeared to drop their demand to be considered as 'special category' prisoners: 'It is wrong for the British government to say that we are looking for different treatment from other prisoners. We would welcome the introduction of the five demands for all prisoners.'

8 July Hunger striker Joe McDonnell died on the 61st day of his fast. A youth was shot dead by the army on the Falls Road. A woman from the Falls Road died after being hit by a plastic bullet near her home.

9 July A youth was shot dead by soldiers under attack on the Crumlin Road, Belfast.

10 July A man was found shot dead in Ballymurphy. At the funeral of Joe McDonnell his young son (who had ended a school essay, in which he had fantasized that his father had escaped, with the words 'and now all the daddies are back with their children') clung to the coffin, weeping, as it was carried out of the house. (18) The media noted that public reaction to the deaths was diminishing; in Dublin, where there had been calls for 'the

86

biggest possible mobilization', only 400 turned out.

13 July Martin Hurson became the sixth hunger striker to die.

16 July In South Armagh a British soldier died following a gun attack on an army post near Crossmaglen.

17 July The Red Cross held talks with the prisoners and with the Secretary of State. The prisoners asked them to withdraw the following day.

21 July A man, apparently mistaken for a member of the UDR, was shot dead in Maghera.

28 July Father Denis Faul, a Dungannon priest, held a meeting with the familes of those on hunger strike where it became clear that most of the families wanted the strike to be called off. Faul contacted Gerry Adams, Vice-President of Sinn Fein, and asked him to get the strike called off. Adams replied that it was the prisoners themselves who wanted it to continue.

29 July Gerry Adams visited the hunger strikers in the Maze, explained to them that the protest was becoming politically ineffective, detailed the concessions the government would grant if the strike was called off, and told them the Republican movement would welcome an end to it. The prisoners refused to call it off.

30 July Relatives of the prisoners said that the IRA should order the hunger strikers to call off their protest.

31 July The Taoiseach Garrett Fitzgerald said that the IRA could bring the hunger strike to an end of they wanted to. In Strabane a former RUC member was shot dead by the INLA. Relatives of hunger striker Patrick Quinn, whose death was imminent, asked doctors to resuscitate him. A few days later when he became lucid his mother took him in her arms and asked, 'Now Paddy, aren't you glad to be alive today?' To which he replied: 'I don't know whether I am or not.' (18)

1 August Kevin Lynch died on his 71st day. Bishop Daly of Derry urged relatives to request that doctors resuscitate unconscious hunger strikers. A man died from injuries received from a plastic bullet.

2 August Kieran Doherty died on his 73rd day. In County Tyrone 2 policemen were killed by a landmine.

5 August The worst spate of bombing for 2 years hit the province.

8 August Hunger striker Tom McElwee died on his 62nd day.

9 August A man died from a plastic bullet injury after rioting in Newtownabbey. A man was shot dead in Ardoyne - the UFF threatened to step up sectarian killings.

11 August A man, thought to have been mistaken for his RUC brother, was shot dead from a motorbike in Belfast.

20 August Michael Devine (INLA) died on his 60th day. He was the 10th hunger striker to die. The family of Patrick McGeown requested medical intervention to save his life. In the new Fermanagh/South Tyrone by-election Owen Carron, standing as an 'Anti-H-Block' candidate, won with 31,278 votes.

1 September Lagan College, an integrated school set up by All Children Together, opened outside Belfast.

2 September Rev. Ian Paisley called for a 'third force' to be set up, on the lines of the former B-Specials.

4 September The family of Matthew Devlin requested medical intervention in order to save his life.

5 September An off-duty soldier was shot dead in the University area of Belfast.

6 September Laurence McKeown, on his 70th day, was given medical treatment at the instigation of his family. An RUC detective was seriously injured after being gunned down leaving Mass in Armagh.

7 September In County Tyrone, 2 teenage policemen were killed by a 700lb landmine on their first patrol.

12 September In Maghera, A UDR member was fatally shot in the back.

88

13 September An RUC Reservist was murdered after visiting his wife (who had just had their second child) at the Mid-Ulster Hospital in Magherafelt.

19 September The UFF murdered a Catholic man on the Ormeau Road, Belfast.

26 September A policeman was shot dead in a public house in Killough, County Down.

27 September Garrett Fitzgerald launched a 'crusade' to alter the Republic's constitution, and what he described as the 'sectarian' nature of Southern society. A youth who the IRA alleged was an informer was found shot dead in Belfast.

28 September A policeman was killed in a rocket attack on his Land Rover.

29 September A part-time UDR member was shot dead by the INLA as he left Mackie's factory in Belfast.

2 October William Craig said that Garrett Fitzgerald's 'crusade' was 'very significant' and criticised James Molyneaux, the OUP leader, for his negative response.

3 October The hunger strike was called off. The Provisionals denounced the role of the Catholic clergy, especially for urging relatives to permit medical intervention. The families of those who had died were left with their memories - when Kieran Doherty's mother was waiting for him to die 'she used to long to take him in her arms and cuddle him and nurse him'. 'But he was such a big strong lad that she felt she could not baby him. And now that he has gone she keeps thinking to herself: "Why didn't I hold him and say I loved him and kiss his cheek with the bones standing out of his face so?" ' (18) Florence Cobb, the wife of a member of the RUC murdered by one of the hunger strikers, said: 'After they die, they will be forgotten, just as those policemen and soliders who died are forgotten after a while, except by those who loved them.'

5 October The *News Letter* pointed out that 64 people had died during the seven months of the hunger strike. A former UDR member was murdered in the grounds of Altnagelvin Hospital in Derry.

6 October The Secretary of State announced changes in the prison regime: all

89

prisoners would be entitled to wear their own clothes; 50% of lost remission would be restored after a prisoner had conformed to prison rules for 3 months; association would be permitted in adjacent wings of the H-Blocks; and more visits would be allowed.

8 October A City councillor who was a hunger strike supporter died in a gun attack on a club in Ardoyne, Belfast.

11 October In London, a nail-bomb attack outside Chelsea Barracks killed one woman and injured 46 soldiers and civilians (a teenager died on the **13th**).

12 October In Belfast the UFF shot dead a Catholic man in his living room.

15 October A woman died after a sectarian attack in the Markets area of Belfast.

16 October A senior UDA Officer was shot dead by the INLA. Sam Duddy, Public Relations Officer for the UDA, appealed for restraint, and said: 'We are totally opposed to sectarian killings.'

17 October In London Sir Stewart Pringle lost a leg after a bomb attack at his home.

19 October In Belfast the UDA blamed the police for shooting dead one of their members at a police check-point.

21 October A part-time UDR sergeant was shot dead by a man disguised as a postman.

26 October In London, a police bomb disposal expert was killed by an IRA bomb in Oxford Street.

28 October In Derry the body of a man was found - the INLA admitted responsibility.

1 November At their ard fheis Provisional Sinn Fein voted against Daithi O'Connaill's *Eire Nua* Federal Ireland policy, but not by the two-thirds majority needed to remove it from the party's manifesto (this was achieved the following year; from now on the emphasis was to be on an all-Ireland state). It was also decided to fight elections and not to abstain from taking local seats in Northern Ireland. Danny Morrison asked the delegates: 'Who

90

here really believes that we can win the war through the ballot-box? But will anyone here object if with a ballot paper in this hand and an Armalite in this hand we take power in Ireland?' The conference was also told that the IRA would escalate its bombing campaign in England.

4 November A UDA member was killed by the UFF, who said he was an informer.

6 November The second Anglo-Irish summit led to the setting-up of an Anglo-Irish inter-governmental Council. Rev. Paisley said it confirmed all his fears.

7 November A 17-year-old boy was killed by a booby-trap car bomb intended for his UDR father.

9 November A part-time UDR member from Lisnaskea was seriously injured and died on the **11th.**

10 November A former UDR man was murdered in the same area where the teenager was killed on the 7th.

12 November An RUC Reservist lost both legs in his booby-trapped car. The Rev. John Batchelor said: 'The time for talking has passed; we cannot allow one more death. I call upon the British government to use the manpower that is available and to legitimately mobilise a third force to smash the terrorism in our midst. The IRA must be put down like the animals that they are.'

14 November The Unionist MP Robert Bradford and a community worker were shot dead by the IRA. A Catholic youth was shot dead in Short Strand, apparently in retaliation; another man who was shot died on the **24th.**

15 November John Hume, at the SDLP's annual conference, claimed the Provisional IRA wanted to provoke civil war.

16 November Rev. Ian Paisley's 'Third Force' made its first appearance when more than 500 men marched in Enniskillen. Paisley said he had despaired of any change coming from Westminster, and called a 'day of action' for the **23rd** - it would include a mass parade of the Third Force in Newtownards. He pledged to make the province ungovernable. Rev. William McCrea, DUP, said: 'We owe it to our children, even if we have to die, to fight the rebels with a Holy determination and never to sheathe the sword until victory is won.'

17 November An off-duty UDR man was shot dead in what the *News Letter* called 'a bid to push Loyalists over the brink'. The Secretary of State, James Prior, was jostled and kicked by an angry crowd at the Dundonald service for Robert Bradford. All over the province towns ground to a halt at memorial services. A tribute read out at some services said: 'The best way we could honour his memory is to forge this day an unbreakable link among all the Unionist people who are prepared to fight and if need be to die to save Ulster from the IRA terrorists and the treachery of the Thatcher administration.' A Catholic man was murdered in Craigavon. An RUC Reservist, wounded 2 months previously, died. The Army announced it was sending in 600 more men.

18 November The UDA withheld its support for Rev. Paisley's 'day of action' and 'Third Force'. A former UDR member was murdered by the IRA. At a press conference Rev. Paisley said: 'We want all political restraints and handcuffs taken off the security forces and a real war carried out against the IRA. They must flush out the Republican enclaves.' He claimed he would teach Mrs. Thatcher a 'severe lesson' on the 23rd, and warned that 'the full orchestra has not been played yet'. He told Loyalists they were in a 'do or die situation'.

19 November A part-time UDR member was murdered in Strabane. The Workers Party warned that the Provisionals were bent on producing a 'river of blood' in Northern Ireland, and pushing the Protestants out of Ulster. The UDA-dominated Ulster Loyalist Central Co-Ordinating Committee decided not to take part in Rev. Paisley's 'day of action'.

20 November The 'day of action' was failing to win outright support from either industrialists or trade union leaders. Rev. Paisley admitted that he had 'taken a risk in calling this day of action. I have staked my credibility on it.' Cardinal Thomas O Fiaich said: 'What we need now is an end to violent deeds before the whole population is engulfed in an orgy of death and destruction.'

21 November. At Newbuildings in County Londonderry guns were produced for the first time at a Third Force demonstration. In Belfast a member of the IRA was arrested by the police after he had been involved in setting up

92

roadblocks. A few days later the man, Christopher Black, was to become the first of a batch of Republican and Loyalist 'supergrasses', who either offered, or were enduced, to give the police information that would implicate over 200 others, in return for immunity from prosecution, and a new life and identity outside Ireland.

22 November A Roman Catholic priest from Strabane who had spoken out against the IRA after the murder of a local UDR man, said he felt 'very emotional' when his 1,500-strong congregation gave him two standing ovations. He said: 'I thought there was a message there for everybody. The congregation were reaching out to the bereaved... they were reaching out to all Protestants to say we want you, we need you, we hope you need us. And I would say to anybody who feels that the culprits are but the tip of an iceberg - there is no iceberg in Ballycolman, the hearts of the people are too warm.'

23 November Rev. Paisley's 'day of action' ended with a mass demonstration by his 'Third Force' in Newtownards. As thousands of men dressed in paramilitary uniforms marched into the centre of the town, Rev. Paisley asked the crowd to 'move out of the way so that I can see my men'. He then said that the speech he was going to make would be the most important announcement Ulster had heard since 1912. ' Fellow Loyalists, this is a very solemn occasion. It is solemn because many of us here tonight will have to lay down our lives to give our children the freedom they deserve. My men are ready to be recruited under the Crown to destroy the vermin of the IRA. But if they refuse to recruit them, then we will have no other decision to make but to destroy the IRA ourselves! We demand that the handcuffs be taken off the security forces! One of my commanders said to me 'any rat will suck eggs in the presence of a chained dog' - that is what the IRA vermin have been doing in the presence of the chained dog of the security forces. If that dog is not unchained, we will be the unchained dog! The killing of the IRA is over as far as Ulster is concerned! We will exterminate the IRA!'

28 November A policeman, who had only been a constable for a few weeks, was killed by an IRA bomb at Unity Flats, Belfast.

9 December Garrett Fitzgerald said that new links with Britain resulting from the Anglo-Irish initiative might help to reassure Unionists. He said the Republic must be prepared to sacrifice its wish to see unity in the immediate future, and wait for it to come by agreement. To facilitate this, articles 2 and 3 of the Constitution should be rewritten.

December This was the first month in 10 years when there were no deaths due to the present 'troubles'.

Death toll for the year: 57 civilians, 10 Army and 34 RUC & UDR.

1982

29 January John McKeague, the well-known Loyalist, was shot dead in his Belfast shop by the INLA.

19 February The De Lorean Motor Cars company went into Receivership. On **24 May** its closure was announced; 1,500 workers were to be laid off on **31 May**. John De Lorean himself was later to be arrested in USA on drugs smuggling charges. On **18 July 1984** a Westminster Public Accounts Committee said that the loss of £77m of taxpayers' money was 'one of the gravest cases of the misuse of public resources for many years'. However they said that the workforce had emerged with credit. On **16 August 1984** John de Lorean was acquitted of drugs charges by a court in Los Angeles, when the jury accepted his plea of 'entrapment' by FBI agents.

8 March The New Ireland Group was formed.

20 March The Provisionals said they would carry out punishment shootings on parents who did not prevent their children engaging in 'criminal activities' in nationalist areas, and revealed they had already shot one parent. On the **31st** they said parents would also be held responsible for any injuries suffered by their children during IRA attacks on the security forces.

5 April The British government published its White Paper on Northern Ireland. James Prior proposed to call elections for a 78-member devolved Assembly elected on a proportional representation system. This in turn would reach agreement on how devolved powers could be exercised, but 70% agreement would be needed for any partial transfer of powers from Westminster.

3 June The Department of the Environment announced that a brick wall, costing £80,000, would be built along the 'peace line' dividing the Falls and Shankill Roads in Belfast.

8 July The preliminary report of the 1981 Census revealed that 133,727 people had left the province since 1971, double the rate for the previous 10 years. The total population was down for the first time in a century to 1,509,892.

15 July Fiona Brown, wife of 'supergrass' Robert Brown and 7 months pregnant, was 'kidnapped'. On the **17 August,** with his wife still missing, Brown withdrew his evidence and charges against 5 men were dropped.

20 July In London, two IRA bombs, one near the barracks of the Household Cavalry in Knightsbridge, the other under a bandstand in Regent's Park, killed 8 people and injured many others (3 more were to die later).

16 September An INLA booby trap bomb in Divis Flats, Belfast, killed a British soldier and 2 local boys, aged 12 and 14. The INLA later expressed its 'deepest sympathy'.

18 October An INLA gunman shot and wounded a 61-year-old headmaster, who had left the UDR 6 years previously, in front of his class of 10-year-olds, who screamed in terror and dived under their desks during the attack.

20 October In the Assembly elections 5 Sinn Fein members were elected, taking 10% of the first preference votes.

22 October After the Provisionals had kidnapped a part-time member of the UDR in South Armagh and said they were holding him for 'interrogation', the PAF kidnapped a Catholic father of 7 in Belfast, holding him as hostage for the UDR man's release. The Catholic was found beaten to death in the lower Shankill area on the **25th.** On the **26th** the IRA claimed it had been unable to prevent the murder of the UDR man because of tight security. On the **29th** the UDR man's body was found, and there was speculation that he had in fact been killed soon after his abduction, but the IRA had delayed revealing the whereabouts of the body in an attempt to conceal the exact time of his murder.

11 November 3 unarmed IRA members were shot dead by police who claimed that the men's car had driven through a checkpoint near Lurgan. The Assembly met for the first time, but the SDLP boycotted it.

16 November Lenny Murphy was shot dead in a Protestant area of Belfast by the IRA. He had recently been released from prison, and was widely believed to be the leader of the 'Shankill Butchers' murder gang. Rumours soon surfaced that Loyalist and Republican paramilitaries had concurred over his assassination.

24 November A 17-year-old Lurgan boy was shot dead and another seriously injured by police who had 'staked out' a farm.

November Father Desmond Wilson and other members of the committee of Springhill Community House in Ballymurphy extended their community outreach by converting a whole floor of a disused mill in Conway Street, off the lower Falls Road, into an education and discussion venue (Conway Mill Community Education Centre). It was soon involved in a wide range of projects, which included drama productions (for which a theatre was built within the complex), seminars, poetry readings, classes for state examinations, and public discussions aimed at promoting community self-awareness and encouraging political dialogue. This year also saw the setting-up of the Rathcoole Self-Help Group, situated in a large Protestant working-class estate to the north of Belfast. The Self-Help Group were to initiate various projects aimed at providing facilities for local residents, especially the growing number of young unemployed. Rathcoole estate, with 14,000 people, didn't possess a single community centre.

6 December The INLA bombed the Droppin' Well, a public house and disco, at Ballygawley in County Londonderry, killing 12 soldiers and 5 civilians, and injuring 66, some seriously. In Belfast, the trial began of 38 people implicated by the testimony of IRA 'supergrass' Christopher Black.

12 December 2 INLA members were shot dead at an RUC checkpoint on the outskirts of Armagh. The shootings, as well as those of the **11th** and **24th** of **November** were to give rise to a 'shoot to kill' controversy.

14 December The Secretary of State admitted that special anti-terrorist squads existed, but denied that they had been given a licence to kill suspects.

22 December After the abduction of Patrick Gilmour in Derry, his family were warned that they would not see him again if his son did not withdraw his evidence against 40 people. The IRA released him on **26 September 1983**.

Death toll for the year: 57 civilians, 21 Army and 19 RUC & UDR.

1983

16 January Judge William Doyle was shot dead by the IRA as he was leaving Mass in Belfast.

11 April 14 men were jailed on the evidence of UVF 'supergrass' Joseph Bennett.

13 April In Dublin the leaders of the 3 main political parties in the Irish Republic met with John Hume, SDLP, with a view to setting up a 'Forum for a New Ireland'. On **30 May** the New Ireland Forum met for its first session.

26 April Rev. Ian Paisley said that 'supergrasses' should first be tried for their own crimes before being allowed to give evidence against others.

9 June UK General Election. Sinn Fein increased their vote to 103,000 (13.4%), and Gerry Adams was elected MP for West Belfast. On the **14th** James Prior said that under no circumstances would he talk to Adams.

5 August 22 people were sentenced on the evidence of 'supergrass' Christopher Black.

9 September 28 people were arrested when Robert Lean became the latest 'supergrass'. On **19 October**, after escaping from police custody, Lean appeared at a Sinn Fein press conference,where he announced he was now retracting his evidence. He was rearrested after the press conference, and the following day charges against 11 people were dropped.

25 September In the biggest escape in British prison history 38 Republican prisoners escaped from the Maze prison. A prison warder was stabbed to death during the escape. 19 men were soon recaptured, but the others made a clear getaway.

24 October 8 men were freed from custody when 'supergrass' Patrick McGurk retracted his evidence.

26 October Gerry Fitt was ennobled as Baron Fitt of Bellshill, after taking the oath of allegiance to the Queen.

13 November Gerry Adams was elected President of Sinn Fein at the party's ard fheis. The outgoing President Ruairi O'Bradaigh along with Daithi O'Connaill resigned from the party executive, leaving the leadership Northern-based.

21 November In South Armagh 3 elders of the Darkley Pentecostal Church near Keady were shot dead by men who claimed to be from the Catholic Reaction Force. On the **27th** Dominic McGlinchey, the alleged Chief-of-Staff of the INLA, admitted in an interview with a Dublin newspaper that the INLA was indirectly involved with the killings. Also on the **27th** Gerry Adams defended as legitimate the killing of British soldiers and RUC members, but condemned the Darkley killings as sectarian.

23 November Lord Justice Gibson threw out the uncorroborated evidence of INLA 'supergrass' Jackie Grimley, saying he considered the witness a liar and a habitual criminal and therefore no reliance could be placed on his evidence.

7 December The OUP's home affairs spokesman, Edgar Graham, was shot dead by the IRA outside Queen's University in Belfast.

17 December An IRA car bomb exploded outside Harrods in London, leaving 8 dead and 80 injured.

Death toll for the year: 41 civilians, 5 Army and 28 RUC & UDR.

1984

9 January A group of DUP Assembly members who had returned from a visit to Israel studying security measures suggested that the border with the Irish Republic should be sealed with a wire fence and electronic surveillance equipment.

January Farset City Farm, one of the schemes initiated by the Farset Youth and

Community Development Project under the management of Jackie Hewitt, Dr. Ian Adamson and others, was opened on waste ground between the Protestant estates of Highfield and Springmartin and the Catholic estates of Ballymurphy, New Barnsley and Moyard. All the buildings on the Farm were built by young people, andmany different animals were housed there. Over the following years hundreds of groups of children from all over Belfast would visit the Farm, most of these children never having been so close to such animals before. In an area noted for its vandalism, the City Farm was never damaged by local youths.

6 March The Assistant-Governor of the Maze prison was shot dead by the IRA.

14 March Gerry Adams and 3 Sinn Fein members were shot and wounded by the UFF as they drove back to the Falls Road after a court appearance in central Belfast.

17 March In the Irish Republic, Dominic McGlinchy was arrested after a shot-out with the Gardai. He was handed over to the RUC a few hours later at the border (the Supreme Court in Dublin had agreed to his extradition on **7 December 1982**). He was the first member of a Republican organisation to be extradited to the North.

29 March An RUC member on trial for the murder of an INLA man on 12 December 1982 claimed that senior officers told him to lie to protect a police informer. He was acquited on **3 April**, when Mr. Justice McDermott ruled that he had acted in self-defence, adding that the claims of a 'cover-up' by the RUC did not concern him. On **7 April** the Chief Constable John Hermon denied there was any cover-up.

6 April The Irish language school in West Belfast was granted maintained status by the Education Minister.

8 April In Belfast the IRA wounded magistrate Thomas Travers and killed his daughter as they were leaving Mass. At the funeral of Mary Travers on the **11th** the Catholic Bishop of Down and Conor Cathal Daly asked people to remember her death when Sinn Fein came looking for their votes.

2 May After hearing numerous submissions the New Ireland Forum came out in favour of Irish unity by consent, but there was no agreement among the main participants as to the structure by which this was to be achieved.

27 May The trial began of 3 RUC members accused of murdering an IRA member on 11 November 1982. On **5 June** Lord Justice Gibson acquitted the men, and praised them for their courage and determination in bringing the IRA members to 'the final court of justice'.

30 May The outspoken Scotsman and Loyalist politician, George Seawright, told a meeting of the Belfast Education and Library Board that Catholics and their priests should be incinerated. On **29 November** he was fined £100 and given a 6-months sentence for his outburst, and on **28 December** was expelled from the DUP.

1 June US President Ronald Regan began a 4-day visit to the Irish Republic. On the **3rd** 10,000 people demonstrated in Dublin against his foreign policies.

14 June In the voting for the European Parliament, Rev. Ian Paisley, John Taylor and John Hume were re-elected. The Sinn Fein vote dropped by 11,000.

28 June 29 people were returned for trial on the evidence of another UVF 'supergrass', James Crockard.

2 July At Westminster the Secretary of State, James Prior, rejected the Irish unity proposals outlined in the report of the New Ireland Forum.

12 August When the banned Noraid spokesman Martin Galvin attempted to speak at a rally outside Sinn Fein headquarters in West Belfast, police advanced through the 2,000-strong crowd to try and arrest him, and in the ensuing violence a man was shot dead by a police plastic bullet.

15 August There were 3 nights of rioting on the Shankill Road in Belfast after UVF 'supergrass' William Allen had implicated 46 men.

22 August The Armagh coroner resigned after seeing police files relating to the shooting of the 2 INLA members on 12 December 1982, saying he found 'grave irregularities' in them. On **3 September** it was announced that the inquest was to be postponed pending the outcome of an investigation into the RUC's role which was to be carried out by officers from the Greater Manchester police force.

July/August The Dutch organisation, Pax Christi Kinderhulp, working jointly with the NSPCC, celebrated its 10th year of taking Protestant and Catholic children to stay with Dutch families for a few weeks each summer. Many European and American organisations regularly organised such holidays.

3 September The British Prime Minister Margaret Thatcher and the Taoiseach Garrett Fitzgerald met in London and announced an Anglo-Irish summit which would be held in **November**.

6 September The British government said it was ceasing its subsidy to the province's gas industry; this would lead to the loss of 1,000 jobs.

21 September 22 people were returned for trial on the testimony of INLA 'supergrass' Harry Kirkpatrick.

29 September In the Irish Republic, 7 ton of arms and ammunition bound for the IRA were seized by police when they boarded the *Marita Ann* off the coast of County Kerry.

12 October In England, an IRA bomb blasted the Grand Hotel, Brighton, where members of the British cabinet were staying for the Conservative Party annual conference. 5 people were killed, and the Prime Minister Margaret Thatcher narrowly escaped injury. A IRA statement said: 'Today we were unlucky, but remember, we only have to be lucky once.'

22 October The European Human Rights Commision dismissed a case brought by the family of a 12-year-old boy killed by a plastic bullet in 1976. The Commision said that as the 99,000 plastic and rubber bullets fired since 1969 had only resulted in 13 deaths, the weapon was not as dangerous as alleged.

19 November Anglo-Irish Summit talks in London. Mrs Thatcher's view of the Summit was that it was a 'full, frank and most realistic meeting'. She had firmly ruled out all of the New Ireland Forum proposals. In Dublin the following day Garrett Fitzgerald was accused of being responsible for the Republic's 'greatest humiliation in recent history', with his 'abject capitulation' to British intransigence.

24 November James Molyneaux told the Unionist Party conference that Mrs. Thatcher had 'slapped down the plotters'. Enoch Powell asserted that she had 'broken out of a viscous spiral planned to create an all-Ireland state'.

25 November The Catholic Bishop of Down and Connor, Cathal Daly, said that

101

failure of the Anglo-Irish dialogue would be too calamitous to contemplate.

4 December The Secretary of State, Douglas Hurd, warned the Northern Ireland Assembly that they would have to make a significant move to accomodate the Nationalist community, otherwise the British government would continue to talk with Dublin over their heads.

18 December The Raymond Gilmour 'supergrass' trial was thrown out of court when Lord Chief Justice Lord Lowry said Gilmour was 'entirely unworthy of belief'. On the **24th** he quashed some of the convictions in another 'supergrass' trial, that involving UVF member Joseph Bennett, saying they were 'unsafe and unsatisfactory'.

Death toll for the year: 36 civilians, 9 Army and 19 RUC & UDR.

1985

23 February John Hume, who, amid much criticism, had accepted a challenge to meet with the Provisionals, walked out of the meeting after a few minutes when the IRA demanded to record part of it on video. In Strabane, 3 members of the IRA were killed by an undercover Army unit.

28 February The Provisionals mortar-bombed Newry RUC station, killing 9 officers. The IRA later announced that any builder involved in repairs to the station would be shot. On **20 May** 4 more RUC officers from Newry were blown up in their patrol car.

22 March The Secretary of State Douglas Hurd and the Foreign Secretary Sir Geoffrey Howe met the Taoiseach Garrett Fitzgerald and the Irish Foreign Minister Peter Barry in Dublin for talks.

17 April The Secretary of State said in Belfast that he might proceed with a new political formula for Northern Ireland even if there was no agreement among the local politicians.

28 April In Limavady Rev. David Armstrong, who had been forced to resign his position following a stormy two-year relationship with church elders opposed to his ecumenical gestures, preached his last sermon. In 1983 and 1984 he had exchanged Christmas greetings with the local Catholic curate and both of them had toured the United States in March to promote reconciliation. The overwhelming support of his congregation was evident by the capacity attendance at the service, and almost every person there shook his hand or embraced him, and many, men included, were in tears. After the service he and 40 members of his church walked across the road to the local Catholic church where many of the Catholic congregation stood in the rain to welcome them and shake hands. When the visitors finally got inside the church the 1,000 people there greeted them with cheers and applause. Rev. Armstrong said that Northern Ireland 'would take people with Christian guts and courage, who are willing to be eaten alive, to bring about reconciliation'. Following his departure a dozen people were to resign their church posts, and many signed a petition calling for the removal of the elders.

15 May In the local government elections, Sinn Fein took 59 out of the 566 seats. On **5 June** a NIO spokesman said that government ministers would neither receive nor correspond personally with Sinn Fein representatives while they refused to renounce violence. Reaction to the appearance of the Sinn Fein members was to lead to repeated disruption in the council chambers around the province. In the elections for the Newtownabbey Borough members of the Rathcoole Self-Help Group put themselves forward as candidates for the All Night Party. One of the candidates, Hagar the Horrible, in his election manifesto, 'promised' to rebuild Stormont in Rathcoole and make it an all-night disco, to hold the next Olympics in Rathcoole, and to tilt the world's axis to give the estate more sunshine. Local Unionist politicians were outraged and repeatedly attacked the Group in the media. The Group responded that the sectarian and corrupt politics of Northern Ireland were a sad joke to start with, so why shouldn't they make it official? They also claimed that the reason the Unionist politicians were so shocked was because they had always had a compliant Protestant electorate, but now young people were fed up and disillusioned. A local DUP councillor claimed the group were 'subversives' and said: 'I think there is only one answer. That is to get a big horse whip and whip them out of the borough once and for all.'

27 June The Secretary of State, Douglas Hurd, said that government funding would be withheld from certain community groups. In a Parliamentary statement he said: 'I am satisfied that there are cases in which some community groups or persons prominent in the direction or management of some community groups, have sufficiently close links with paramilitary organisations to give rise to a grave risk that to give support to these groups would have the effect of improving the standing and furthering the aims of a paramilitary organisation, whether directly or indirectly.' Although no specific charges were made or substantiated, several community groups had funding withdrawn, including the Conway Mill Education Centre (which said it would continue without funding). When an SDLP councillor in **February 1986** accused unnamed community centres in West Belfast of being 'paramilitary fronts', community activists replied that middle-class interests in the Catholic Churh and the SDLP, in alliance with the British government, were trying to stiffle all attempts by working-class people to take control of their own affairs and initiate political dialogue.

12 July Rioting erupted in Portadown when a large force of police prevented the annual Orange parade from going through the Catholic Obin Street area.

1 September Hazelwood Integrated Schools opened in North Belfast; the Primary received maintained status in **January 1987**, the College in **June 1988**.

18 September The report of the investigation by the deputy Chief Constable of Greater Manchester into the RUC operations in Armagh in 1982, which resulted in 6 IRA and INLA members being killed, was presented to the Chief Constable Sir John Herman. On **25 October** the report was handed over to the Director of Public Prosecutions.

24 September The Secretary of State called for an end to speculation about the talks with Dublin. Peter Robinson said that the DUP and the OUP had agreed to a plan of resistance to oppose any settlement they couldn't accept.

8 October The court of Appeal in Belfast quashed the conviction against Dominic McGlinchy, much to the embarrassment of the police. McGlinchy was rearrested after the court and on the **11th** was re-extradited to the Irish Republic, to face charges relating to the shoot-out when he was first apprehended there.

15 October Larne priest Father Pat Buckley, who had been outspoken on social and security issues, was dismissed from his post by Bishop Cathal Daly. On the **20th** he announced he had begun legal proceedings for unfair dismissal. He was also refusing to vacate the church's house in Larne.

November Father Des Wilson's book, *An End to Silence*, was published. In it he said: 'The citizens of Northern Ireland are victims of decisions and choices carefully made by their religious and political leaders. These leaders did not fail. They succeeded. There lies the tragedy of the place.'

2 November The United Ulster Loyalist Front issued a call to form 'Ulster Clubs' throughout Northern Ireland to resist any Anglo-Irish deal.

3 November The Sinn Fein ard fheis rejected a motion backed by the northern leadership that the policy of abstention from the Dail be changed from its status as a principle to that of a tactic.

15 November The Anglo-Irish Agreement was signed at Hillsborough in County Down between the British Prime Minister Margaret Thatcher and the Taoiseach Garrett Fitzgerald amid very tight security. In the agreement the Republic was given a strong consultative role in Northern Ireland affairs through an Inter-governmental Conference, which would be serviced by a full-time Secretariat of British and Irish civil servants. On the **21st** in Dublin the Dail accepted the agreement, and on the **27th** the House of Commons at Westminster approved it also.

20 November The Secretary of State, Tom King, was assaulted by an angry crowd of Loyalists when he arrived for a luncheon at Belfast City Hall.

23 November A massive Loyalist demonstration against the Agreement took place outside Belfast City Hall, with the estimates of people attending varying from 40,000 to 100,000. No Unionist politicians had been party to any of the discussions leading up to the Agreement, nor had they been consulted regarding it.

11 December The first session of the Anglo-Irish conference was held amid tight security at Stormont castle. 2,000 workers marched in protest to Maryfield, the site of the Anglo-Irish Secretariat outside Belfast, and violence erupted when some of the crowd attacked police guarding the gates. Father Des Wilson said: 'Just as Margaret Thatcher does not speak for the working-class Protestants of the Shankill and East Belfast, neither does Garrett Fitzgerald speak for the Catholic working class of Ballymurphy.'

105

17 December All 15 Unionist MP's resigned their seats at Westminster to force by-elections (when the by-elections were held in **January** one of the seats was lost to Seamus Mallon of the SDLP, and the Sinn Fein vote slumped).

18 December 25 men were convicted at Belfast court on the evidence of INLA 'supergrass' Harry Kirkpatrick.

Death toll for the year: 25 civilians, 2 Army, and 27 RUC & UDR.

1986

2 February Peter Robinson, DUP, said that the Anglo-Irish Agreement had to go but he agreed with a suggestion made by Harold McCusker, OUP, that a tripartite conference of British, Irish and Northern Irish politicians should discuss the 'totality of relationships' within the two islands.

3 March A Loyalist 'day of action' against the Anglo-Irish Agreement ended in widespread rioting in Protestant areas, with hooded youths burning out cars and snipers firing on the RUC.

31 March Loyalist gangs attacked Catholic homes in Lisburn, County Down, with stones and petrol-bombs. There were riots in Portadown when Loyalists attacked the RUC after an Apprentice Boys' parade was banned (the next day a man who was injured and later died became the first Protestant to be killed by a plastic bullet). Loyalists also continued with their attacks on the homes of RUC members, accusing the RUC of being prepared to implement the decisions of Dublin through the Anglo-Irish Agreement.

20 May As the attacks on the homes of RUC members escalated, the government revealed at Westminster that there had been 368 cases of intimidation on RUC members and their families since the signing of the Agreement.

5 June John Stalker was removed from the inquiry into the allegations of an RUC 'shoot to kill'·policy. He was later accused of having associated with known criminals in Manchester, and although cleared of these allegations on **22 August** he was not returned to the RUC inquiry. His place was taken by the West Yorkshire Chief Constable Colin Samson.

23 June The Northern Ireland Assembly was officially dissolved. 22 members, mostly from the DUP, refused to leave, and police eventually had to drag them away the next morning.

1 July After the people of the Republic (in the Divorce Referendum in **June**) had voted by 63.5% to keep the constitutional ban on divorce, a spokesman for the Workers' Party (the political party formed from the Republican Clubs) said the result was a bitter blow to the struggle for basic democratic secular politics, which would enforce in many minds in Northern Ireland that the Republic in reality was 'the fiefdom of medieval clerical princes'. He added: 'It must be said that the statements made by the Catholic clerical spokespersons to the (New Ireland) Forum on the principle of the separation of Church and State are now clearly seen to have been nothing more than lip serivce.' Rev. Ian Paisley said: 'In the providence of God, this has brought us back from the brink. If the referendum had been a success the British government would have pushed us with more vigour down the United Ireland road. The civil war, which I believed was at hand, had receded because of that.'

2 July 4 members of the UDR were sentenced to life imprisonment for the murder of a Catholic man as he walked home from work in November 1983.

3 July The Taoiseach, Garrett Fitzgerald, while convinced he was right to put the divorce referendum to the Irish people, and was critical of the 40% of voters who abstained, admitted that the result was 'something of a setback to the long-term prospect of the two parts of Ireland coming closer together politically'. 'It cannot reasonably be denied that we have a long way to go before we create in this part of Ireland a society that would seem welcoming to, open to, and attractive to people of the Northern Unionist tradition.'

6 July Orangemen clashed with the RUC in Portadown after a large force of police sought to allow only members of the Portadown lodge admittance to the 'Tunnel', the entrance to the Nationalist Obin Street area. An SDLP representative said afterwards: 'It is simply intolerable that the Nationalist population of Portadown should be held ransom in their own homes for most of the day in order to allow a totally unnecessary exercise in coat-trailing and deliberate provocation by Loyalists.'

11/16 July There was a week of rioting in Protestant areas of Belfast and Portadown. On the **14th** Catholic homes in Rasharkin, County Antrim, were attacked by 50 Loyalists armed with cudgels and hatchets. The Secretary of State later described the Rasharkin attacks as some of the nastiest and most viscious that had taken place throughout what he called 'the emergency'.

17 July The Appeal court quashed the convictions on 18 of the men named by IRA 'supergrass' Christopher Black.

19 July A Catholic man was the latest victim in a resurgence of killing by Loyalist murder gangs in North Belfast. At the man's funeral on the **22nd** the Catholic Bishop of Down and Conor, Cathal Daly, said he refused to call the murderers 'Protestants'. 'The name 'Protestant' is the name of an honourable religious tradition which has enriched history and which stands for all that is best and noblest in the beliefs and values of millions of Christians. I am confident that both our communities will draw back from the brink. I believe neither community will allow false leaders to drag them to ruin.' On the **27th**, commenting on the murder of 3 RUC officers in Newry, he said their killing was 'simply a continuation of sectarian conflict'.

28 July The Provisional IRA issued a threat to those civilians working in RUC and Army barracks. They said that previous warnings had been ignored and they would not issue any more but would take action against those they accused of collaboration with the security forces. A Sinn Fein councillor said: 'These civilians, whether pushing pens or pushing brooms, permit by their activites the release of British Army and UDR personnel from these tasks and enable them to carry out patrol duties. They are therefore as culpable in their employment practices as they would be if they were directly involved in the manufacture of plastic bullets, and there is no distinction in the reality as experienced by Nationalists.' In response to the threat, a Workers' Party representative in Derry said: 'They wish to dictate to people about every aspect of their lives. They wish to tell where and when they can work; where they can live; if they are to be let live. They are fascists and must be rejected totally by all decent people in this country.' On the **30th** the IRA killed a Protestant business contractor in Greencastle, County Tyrone, saying they had 'executed' him for supplying the security forces.

5 August In a further statement, the IRA said it wanted to clarify 'once and for all' who was considered a legitimate murder target. Their list of people and businesses who were 'part of the war machine' by their work for the security forces, and who therefore would be 'treated as collaborators' who 'must expect to suffer the consequences', included building contractors; civil servants; fuel, food and cleaning contractors; British Telecom; Standard Telephones; shipping and bus companies who transported soldiers and UDR members; and vending machine suppliers. Sinn Fein spokesmen gave the statement their backing, Danny Morrison saying it was 'understood and appreciated' by Nationalists. The SDLP deputy leader Seamus Mallon claimed it was 'a declaration of murderous violence against the community itself'. On the **27th** the IRA further warned doctors, solicitors and clergymen who had to visit RUC bases to display 'appropriate signs' on their vehicles, and added: 'Finally we take this opportunity to warn local car dealers that they are to make potential car buyers aware of any vehicle that has previously been owned by Crown Forces.' An SDLP spokesman commented that the Provisionals' definition of legitimate target was 'getting ever wider'. On the **28th** a young Protestant electrician was shot dead in Derry by the IRA while he waited in his car for his father. The IRA said their victim had worked as an electrician in a local UDR base.

7 August In the Republic, Peter Robinson, DUP, was arrested after 500 Loyalists had 'invaded' Clontibret just across the border in County Monaghan, assaulted two members of the Gardai, and marched through the village in military formation.

3 September Harold McCusker, OUP, said that because of the Anglo-Irish Agreement the Union with Britain was not worth fighting for, much less dying for. On the **9th** Peter Robinson, DUP, agreed that Unionists might now have to consider Independence.

11 September Robert McCartney, a Belfast lawyer, stressed the need for 'equal citizenship': 'Either the people of Northern Ireland are British citizens entitled to equal citizenship or they are not.' (The 'equal citizenship' lobby were hoping to rectify the anomaly whereby both the British Conservative and Labour Parties don't permit local constituency organisations to be set up in Northern Ireland. Those seeking 'equal citizenship' felt that this prohibition left people in Northern Ireland unable to vote on the major left/ right political issues that were paramount in the rest of the UK, and so stultified political allegiances in the province along traditional sectarian lines.)

14 September John Bingham, a UVF commander, was assassinated by the IRA who claimed he had been behind recent sectarian murders of Catholics. His funeral was attended by Loyalist politicians.

2 November The Sinn Fein ard fheis voted by a two-thirds majority to drop its abstentionist policy in the Republic against taking seats in the Dail. Ruairi O'Bradaigh, Daithi O'Connaill and 100 others walked out in protest. 'With their departure passed the last traces of the old Southern Provisional leadership.' (2)

15 November Following a massive demonstration at Belfast City Hall against the Anglo-Irish Agreement a section of the crowd damaged 70 shops and looted some of them.

24 November Newspaper reports claimed that the Samson report would recommend that 8 RUC officers be prosecuted for conspiring to pervert the course of justice during the inquiry into the 'shoot-to-kill' controversy.

23 December 24 Belfast men convicted on the word of 'supergrass' Harry Kirkpatrick were freed after their convictions were quashed.

Death toll for the year: 37 civilians, 4 Army and 20 RUC & UDR.

1987

3 January Leaders of the OUP and DUP launched a petition calling for a referendum on the Anglo-Irish Agreement. In London on **14 February** the petition, which contained 400,000 names and was to be given to the Queen, was handed in at Buckingham Palace.

29 January The UDA published a new political document, drawn up by John McMichael and other members of the organisation. Entitled *Common Sense* it proposed a devolved government for Northern Ireland with a written constitution, its structure based on consensus government, proportional representation and shared responsibility. It added: 'There is no section of this divided Ulster community which is totally innocent or indeed totally guilty, totally right or totally wrong. We all share the responsibility for creating the situation, either by deed or by acquiescence. Therefore we must share the responsibility for finding a settlement and then share the responsibility of maintaining good government.'

110

24 February The DUP and the OUP announced the setting up of a 'Task Force' to look into political alternatives to the Anglo-Irish Agreement.

14 March The leader of the INLA army council was murdered in the middle of a feud within the organisation that eventually led to 16 deaths.

17 March President Ronald Regan confirmed US backing for the Anglo-Irish Agreement when he authorized the first $50m grant to the International Fund for Ireland set up in conjunction with the Agreement.

22 March In an interview with the *Sunday Times,* a man who claimed to be a former MI5 agent said that British Intelligence had tried to destabilise Harold Wilson's Labour government through activities in Ireland. Other Army personnel were to make similar allegations.

23 March The Chief Constable Sir John Hermon received the second report on the alleged 'shoot to kill' policy, this time from John Stalker's replacement, Colin Sampson.

25 April Lord Justice Gibson, Northern Ireland's second most senior judge, and his wife were killed driving back from Dublin when the IRA detonated a bomb in a stationary car parked at the roadside.

1 May Sinn Fein presented their proposals *Scenario for Peace*, in which they demanded that Britain withdraw from Ireland, and called for an all-Ireland constitutional conference.

8 May After bombing the police station at Loughgall, County Armagh, 8 members of the IRA were killed by members of the SAS and RUC who had been lying in wait for them.

12 June In a UK General Election the vote for Sinn Fein dropped from 13.4% (in 1983) to 11.3%. Gerry Adams retained his West Belfast seat. The SDLP won 3 seats.

16 August Rev. Ian Paisley reaffirmed that the Agreement had to be suspended before inter-party talks could take place.

1 November In France 150 ton of guns and ammunition, including 20 surface-to-air missiles, bound for the IRA from Lybia were seized on the *Eksund* at

Brest harbour.

8 November While hundreds of people were gathered in the centre of Enniskillen for a remembrance-day service for the dead of two world wars, an IRA bomb exploded killing 11 and injuring 63, 19 very seriously. The atrocity stunned the nation, both North and South of the border. The IRA later issued a statement in which they said they 'deeply regret what occurred'. The murders became known as the 'poppy-day massacre'.

19 November Loyalist George Seawright was shot dead by the Irish People's Liberation Organisation (a splinter group from the INLA) - he died on **3 December**.

3 December In the Republic a new Extradition Act was passed in the Dail, with an amendment that the attorney-general must satisfy himself that there was a case to be answered before permitting any extradition request to proceed.

22 December The UDA's second-in-comand, John McMichael, was assassinated by the IRA. The Chief Constable of the RUC was later to hint at 'collusion' between vested interests within the paramilitaries - McMichael had said publicly that he would be investigating racketeering within the organisation. McMichael was one of a number of Protestant working-class leaders (men like Ernest Elliott, Sammy Smyth, and John McKeague) who although they had started off as 'hard-line', even bigoted, Loyalists, had over the years developed a cross-community consciousness and sought some form of contact, even rapprochement, with the Catholic community, but had been murdered either by Republicans or fellow Loyalists.

Death toll for the year: 66 civilians, 3 Army and 24 RUC & UDR.

1988

11 January John Hume of the SDLP and Gerry Adams, Sinn Fein, met for the first of a series of meetings, a move which attracted widespread criticism.

25 January The attorney-general Sir Patrick Mayhew announced that the 11

RUC officers named in the Stalker/Sampson 'shoot-to-kill' investigation would not be prosecuted for reasons of 'national security'. This decision was widely criticised by Nationalist politicians North and South, and by Labour MP's at Westminster.

28 January   In London the Court of Appeal rejected a plea from the 'Birmingham Six' against their convictions for the Birmingham bombings in November 1974. They claimed that their confessions were made after they had been beaten up by the police. On **1 December 1986** a TV documentary had cited a former Birmingham police officer who agreed the 6 had been assaulted.

6 March 3 IRA members were killed in Gibraltar by an army undercover team who had been shadowing them, and had reason to believe a bomb had been planted. A government statement said that when an attempt had been made to arrest the 3, they had made moves that seemed to put the lives of the soliders and civilians in danger, so they were shot. The 3 were found to be unarmed.

11 March Andy Tyrie, Chairman of the UDA, resigned after failing to get a vote of confidence from the organisation's Inner Council. On the **7th** a bomb had been found under his car, believed to have been placed there by Loyalists.

14 March At a UDA press conference a message from the UFF was read out, claiming that 'innocent Catholics' had nothing to fear from the organisation. The following day the UFF shot dead a Catholic trade union official.

16 March At Milltown cemetery in Belfast 3 men were shot dead by a lone Loyalist gunman who attacked the funerals of the 3 IRA members killed in Gibraltar.

19 March 2 British soldiers who unaccountably drove into the path of the funeral procession for one of the victims of the Loyalist gunman, were attacked by a crowd of men, badly beaten, and then shot dead by members the IRA.

1 May 3 members of the Royal Air Force were murdered in Holland by the IRA in two separate attacks.

15 May 3 Catholic men were shot dead in a Belfast bar by the UVF.

19 May An IRA bomb went off at the RUC stand at the Balmoral Show in Belfast, injuring 13, including children getting ice cream nearby. A Sinn Fein spokesman later said that 'people have been told not to go near the police'.

25 May The government published its White Paper on fair employment practices.

15 June 6 British soliders taking part in a charity fun-run in Lisburn were killed by the IRA when a bomb exploded under their minibus.

7 July 2 civilians were killed on the Falls Road in Belfast by an IRA bomb intended for the security forces.

23 July A family of 3 from Hillsborough were killed near Newry by an IRA bomb intended for 'Crown forces'. The IRA said the deaths were a 'tragic mistake'.

July A joint statement issued by West Belfast Community Groups accused the International Fund for Ireland of reinforcing the present system of economic inequality, and of furthering and promoting 'sectarian divisions in Northern Ireland by selectively funding the commercial interests of Catholic Church authorities and their political and business associates'.

4 August Two elderly Protestants were murdered by the IRA because they had been repairing Belleck RUC station. An article in the *Belfast Telegraph* later said: 'Someone said that Irish nationalism consists not of love of one's country but of hatred of someone else's. "Their moving spirit," he said, "is not love of Ireland, but hatred of Britain." If this is so, it may go some way towards explaining the frightfulness of the IRA onslaught on the citizens of this part of the island. The depth of the hatred they feel must be so intense as to suppress the normal instinct of revulsion which would restrain other people, however motivated, from firing 150 automatic rifle bullets into two blameless and defenceless men as they made their way home after a hard day's work in County Fermanagh.' The article went on to say that the killing afterwards of two Catholic men in Belfast by Loyalists was an 'equally callous murder'. 'There can be no excuse for the savagery.'

20 August 8 young British soldiers were killed and many were injured in an IRA bomb attack on their bus in County Tyrone.

4 September A march took place from Coalisland to Dungannon to celebrate the 20th anniversary of the first Civil Rights March. Gerry Adams said the Northern Ireland state was on 'a life-support machine'. A new group, the '68 Committee, unfurled a banner which read: 'No Civil Rights without National Rights'. Austin Currie, who had organised the 1968 march didn't attend, but instead 'congratulated' the people of Coalisland and Dungannon for 'their good sense in ignoring today's attempt to rewrite history'. In Derry, at the funeral of 2 old-age-pensioners killed by another IRA 'mistake bomb', Martin McGuiness of Sinn Fein was shouted at as he left the church, and an angry mourner criticised him for attending Mass.

8 October A march took place in Derry along the same route taken twenty years before by the first Civil Rights march in the city on 5 October 1968. Gerry Adams, President of Sinn Fein, addressing the crowd, said: 'Twenty years is twenty years too many. It is time (the British) left, and they will not leave until we push them home. We have nowhere to go but forward. They have nowhere to go but home.' Eamonn McCann, one of the organisers of the 1968 march (and one of those who had 'argued down the proposed (NICRA) invitation to the Unionists' to participate in the original march (3)), told the crowd: 'All the sectarianism came from the bigoted Unionist state, none of it came from those who marched on October 5 and we accept responsibility for none of it. The dam that burst twenty years ago was a dam of bigotry that had been fashioned not by us - but by the State.' A gathering of Loyalists had been kept away from the march by the RUC, and at one stage some of the crowd unsuccessfully tried to lift Rev. Ian Paisley onto the bonnet of a police Land Rover to wave a Union Jack defiantly at the marchers. (On **12 October** Rev. Paisley was to be ejected from the European Parliament at Strasbourg after interrupting the Pope's address, calling him the 'Anti-Christ'.) In Belfast, a woman in Ballymurphy said: 'I don't know what there is to celebrate about. Between the lot of them - the Brits, the Loyalists, and our crowd - they've wasted twenty years of our lives.'

Death toll to 5 August: 27 civilians, 12 Army and 13 RUC & UDR.

Abbreviations

CCDC	Central Citizens' Defence Committee
DUP	Democratic Unionist Party
GOC	General Officer Commanding
INLA	Irish National Liberation Army
IRSP	Irish Republican Socialist Party
LAW	Loyalist Association of Workers
NICRA	Northern Ireland Civil Rights Association
NIO	Northern Ireland Office
OUP	Official Unionist Party
PAF	Protestant Action Force
PD	People's Democracy
RUC	Royal Ulster Constabulary
SDLP	Social Democratic and Labour Party
UDA	Ulster Defence Association
UDR	Ulster Defence Regiment
UFF	Ulster Freedom Fighters
USC	Ulster Special Constabulary
UVF	Ulster Volunteer Force
UWC	Ulster Workers' Council

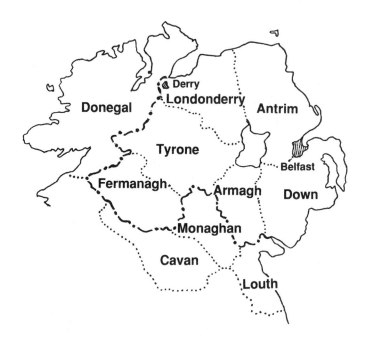

In this chronology Northern Ireland is sometimes referred to by Nationalist spokesmen as the 'Six Counties', and the Republic of Ireland as the 'Twenty-six Counties'. While the term 'Ulster' is used by most people to mean the political entity of Northern Ireland, many Nationalists feel that it should only be applied to the 'province' of Ulster, which has a total of nine counties, three of them in the Irish Republic. Ironically the configuration they usually refer to - the six counties within Northern Ireland, plus counties Donegal, Monaghan and Cavan in the Republic - is itself an English invention, for what could be described as the 'ancient province of Ulster', dating from the dawn of Ireland's written history right up to the Anglo-Irish and Gaelic Lordships in the late 16th Century, included the territory now in County Louth rather than Cavan. It was Queen Elizabeth I's administrators who decided to add Louth to the province of Leinster, and give the territory now in Cavan to the province of Ulster.

The town of Derry became Londonderry on 29 March 1613, but most people in Northern Ireland, including most Protestants, still prefer to use the shorter name. County Londonderry on the other hand was an artificial entity when it was established in 1613, and the area it comprises had never been known as Derry or by any one Irish name before the city of London's connection with it.

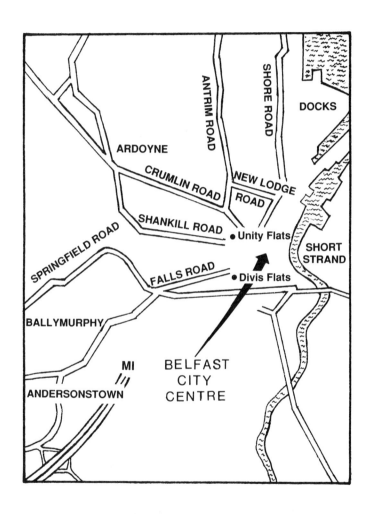

ANTRIM ROAD

SHORE ROAD

DOCKS

ARDOYNE

CRUMLIN ROAD

NEW LODGE
ROAD

SHANKILL ROAD

● Unity Flats

SPRINGFIELD ROAD

SHORT
STRAND

FALLS ROAD

● Divis Flats

BALLYMURPHY

MI

BELFAST
CITY
CENTRE

ANDERSONSTOWN

Sources

For anyone studying Northern Ireland events, the early years (1968-1974) are covered in an exhaustively detailed chronology compiled by Richard Deutsch and Vivien Magowen (**1**). The three volumes of this work are an indispensable guide to that period, and the two authors offer it 'to future scribes and historians' in the hope that it will be 'of assistance' to them. I only hope that some day they consider continuing with their labours.

Fortnight magazine has been, without a doubt, the most important publication to appear in Northern Ireland over the last twenty years. Not only has it provided in-depth analysis of the turmoil Northern Irish society has gone through, but it has managed to get many of the main participants to regularly express their views through its pages. One important aspect of the magazine has been the inclusion of an 'Events Diary' in each issue: this was certainly a far-sighted decision by the editor, but perhaps even he didn't realise just how 'far' he would have to continue with it. From my own point of view, when sitting day after day in the Linen Hall Library going through innumerable, and already disintegrating, copies of the *Belfast Telegraph*, the *News Letter* and the *Irish News*, it was a relief at times to 'escape' to the columns of *Fortnight* for guidance.

Many of the events that were reported in the newspapers of the day have been subsequently analysed by countless historians and investigative journalists. Where these authors have shed light on details that were not public knowledge at the time, I have included such details, and have indicated the source with a number in brackets.

1   *Northern Ireland, 1968-74; A Chronology of Events*, 3 vols, Richard Deutsch and Vivien Magowen, Blackstaff Press, 1975.
2   *The Provisional IRA*, Patrick Bishop and Eamonn Mallie, Corgi Books, 1988.
3   *War and an Irish Town*, Eamonn McCann, Pluto Press, 1980.
4   *The Price of my Soul*, Bernadette Devlin, Pan Books, 1969.
5   *Burntollet*, Bowes Egan and Vincent McCormack, L.R.S. Publishers, 1969.
6   *Ulster*, The Sunday Times Insight Team, Penguin Books, 1972.
7   *The People's Democracy, 1968-73*, Paul Arthur, Blackstaff Press, 1974.

8   *The Narrow Ground*, A.T.Q. Stewart, Pretani Press, 1986.
9   *The UVF, 1966-73*, David Boulton, Torc Books, 1973.
10   *Ireland-A Terrible Beauty*, Jill and Leon Uris, Corgi Books, 1978.
11   *Political Murder in Northern Ireland*, Martin Dillon and Denis Lehane, Penguin Books, 1973.
12   *The Centre Cannot Hold*, Tom Collins, Bookworks Ireland, 1983.
13   *The Churches in Northern Ireland*, Belfast Workers Research Unit, 1980.
14   *The Fall of the Executive*, Paddy Devlin, 1975.
15   *The Point of No Return*, Robert Fisk, Times Books, 1975.
16   *The Cruthin, The Identitiy of Ulster*, and *Bangor-Light of the World*, Ian Adamson, Pretani Press, various dates.
17   *Ulster's Uncertain Defenders*, Sarah Nelson, Appletree Press, 1984.
18   *Ten Men Dead-the story of the 1981 Irish Hunger Strike*, David Beresford, Grafton Books, 1987.